CARD GAMES
UP-TO-DATE
THE STANDARD WORK

by

CHARLES ROBERTS

AUTHOR OF "HOW TO WIN AT CARDS", ETC., ETC.

LONDON
W. FOULSHAM & CO. LTD
NEW YORK   TORONTO   CAPE TOWN   SYDNEY

W. FOULSHAM & CO. LTD.
Yeovil Road, Slough, Berks., England.

ISBN 0-572-00001-4

Printed in Great Britain by
Compton Printing Ltd., Aylesbury
Copyright by
W. FOULSHAM & CO. LTD.

PREFACE

THIS book is not written for the "expert". It is written in plain English for the plain man who enjoys a game of cards as a relaxation.

Care has been taken to make the details and rules correct and in accordance with the accepted standard or recognised code.

Nearly fifty well-known games are dealt with and hints are given which will enable a novice to hold his own after a reasonable amount of practice, and which may also be followed with profit by the seasoned player.

Card games fall into certain well-defined groups or families; and for the benefit of those wishing to learn new games, the simplest of each group is described first and the more complicated afterwards. The descriptions of the manner in which the games are played have been so arranged that new players may adopt the childlike but eminently common-sense method of sitting down to play with the book in hand—following the process in practice, as it is described; and to make the descriptions clear, all "technical" terms are explained beforehand.

Owing to considerations of space some of the matter is perforce somewhat condensed; but the writer trusts, and is fairly confident, that in no case has clarity been sacrificed to brevity.

CHARLES ROBERTS

CONTENTS

CARD GAMES UP-TO-DATE

PART 1

THE BEST CARD GAMES

INTRODUCTION

IT is a very rare thing to meet anyone who has not at least a slight knowledge of card play. Most people know the names of the cards and suits, and how to play some game or other. Nevertheless, there are some who have no such knowledge; and for these the following elementary information is given.

An ordinary pack of cards consists of fifty-two cards, arrayed in a series of four suits, thirteen of each. The suits

FIG. 1.—The five best cards of the Heart suit

are Clubs, Diamonds, Hearts and Spades. Hearts and Diamonds are red, and Clubs and Spades are black—merely for the purpose of making them easily distinguishable.

The best card of a suit is usually the Ace, the unit; following which, in this order, come the King, Queen,

7

Jack, ten, nine, and so on down to the two, which is the lowest card in the suit. Fig. 1 shows a "hand" of five cards, comprising the five best Hearts. In certain games, however, the Ace merely counts as a one, and is the least valuable card in the suit. On these occasions the King occupies his rightful position.

For some games there are additions made to the pack, for other games some of the cards are taken out. For example: The poker pack has a "joker" (sometimes called "mistigris"), a fifty-third card, added. (See Fig. 2.)

FIG. 2.—The Joker ("Mistigris")

This is the most valuable card, as it can be made to represent anything, an Ace or a King, or an extra ten or Jack, or whatever may be wanted. For the game known as Euchre the joker is used, but all the small cards below the seven are thrown out.

Usually the various suits are all of the same value—the Ace of Hearts is of no more worth than the Ace of Spades. But in some games the suits vary in value; for instance, in Contract Bridge the suits rank in the order of Clubs, Diamonds, Hearts and Spades—the last-named being the highest.

In games of the "Whist" variety (Nap, Solo, Contract Bridge, and some others) it is part of the game to make one of the suits a "trump" suit. This means that a particular suit is for a certain time (usually, but not always, for one "hand") better than any of the other three suits, which remain of equal value amongst themselves. Thus if Hearts are trumps *any* Heart is better than *any* card of the other suits, e.g. a two of Hearts will beat an Ace of Spades. Of course one trump card will beat another if it is higher, e.g. the three of trumps would beat the two.

Cards are generally dealt one by one to each player, after being shuffled (that is, well mixed together) by one player, and cut (some taken from the top and placed underneath) by another player. The dealer deals the first card to the player on his left, and so on, in the way that the hands of a clock go; the last card then falls to the dealer.

It is customary to "cut" or "draw" before play begins, to decide on partners if it is a partnership game, and on who shall deal the first hand. Once this has been decided, in most games each player deals in turn, the rotation being in a clockwise direction. Thus the second hand is dealt by the player sitting on the left of the dealer of the first hand, the third hand by the player sitting on the left of the second dealer, and so on.

Modern games like Contract Bridge and Canasta include drawing or cutting in the official rules. It is laid down that the players drawing the two highest cards play against those who draw the two lowest cards; and the player drawing the highest card deals the first hand. Ace counts as the highest card, and where two or more cards of the same denomination are turned up, they rate according to suit value in the order (from highest to lowest) Spades, Hearts, Diamonds, Clubs. So, for example, the nine of clubs is higher than the eight of spades, but the eight of spades is higher than the eight of clubs.

In other games, especially the older ones, the custom is for the player who cuts the *lowest* card to win the deal; and in many such games Ace is counted as the lowest card, not the highest. As the nature of the cut does not affect the play it does not matter which order is adopted; but it is advisable to secure agreement before the first cut is made.

The player sitting immediately on the dealer's left hand is almost invariably the first to play in the "hand". A "hand" of cards, be it noted, means in this sense the whole of the play of the cards dealt, until another deal is required; in another sense, the term "hand" is used to indicate all the cards dealt to a player, i.e., the cards he holds in his hand.

The first player, sitting on the dealer's left, is known as the "eldest hand".

In most games the player's object is to win "tricks". A trick is a round of cards in which all the players play one card (unless the rules of the game prevent one or more of them from playing in that particular trick). The most valuable card played—according to the rules of whatever game is in progress—wins the trick; and the player of that card not only scores the trick but has, usually, the privilege of "leading" (playing first) in the next trick.

Some other common expressions in connection with card games which a novice should note are:—

"Court Cards": Strictly speaking the King, Queen, and Jack; but sometimes used to include the Ace and ten.

"Honours": The Ace, King, Queen, Jack, and (sometimes) ten (used in Whist, Contract Bridge, etc.).

"Knave": An obsolete name for the Jack. In English packs the third court card is marked "J".

"Deuce": A slang term for the two of any suit.

"Tray": A slang term for the three of any suit.

"Revoke": Failure (intentional or otherwise) to play a card of the suit led by first player, when the rules provide that such card shall be played if held.

"Singleton": One card only of a suit, as originally dealt.

A few words on the etiquette of card play may also be useful. All the better-known games have more or less elaborate codes of rules which provide for every circumstance, and if the player abides by these he cannot go wrong. The average card player is, however, human, and does not usually know all the rules—much less keep them.

A golden rule is to suit your behaviour to the company. Card playing is, after all, a pastime, and really need not be treated as though the game were a matter of life or death. Nevertheless, if by ill fortune you play with those who treat it as such, then of course you should not offend them by chatting volubly throughout the game. For, strictly speaking, silence, except for the words of the game, is supposed to be observed by all, in all games.

NAPOLEON

"NAP," as it is familiarly called, is still one of the most popular card games in this country. It is related to Whist, though whether as an ancestor or a descendant it would be difficult to say.

Nap is somewhat simpler to learn than Whist, and much simpler than Contract Bridge; and it is placed first in this book, and described at some length, because it forms a useful introduction to both these games—indeed, to all games of the Whist type.

It must not be inferred that it is child's play: to play Nap well requires a high degree of judgment and skill.

It is played with a full pack of fifty-two cards and is a good fast game, for three or more players up to seven. Five makes the best number. It is usually played for so much a trick, a penny, or less or more, as may be agreed among the players. Counters or "chips" may be conveniently used, bought from time to time from one player acting as banker, and "cashed" with him at the end of the game.

The cards rank as at Whist, Ace highest and two lowest. The first deal is determined by turning up a card in front of each of the players, when the lowest turned up indicates the first dealer. The Ace is in this case regarded as the lowest card. When it has been decided who is to deal, the player on the dealer's left shuffles the cards, and the dealer may shuffle them after him if he chooses. They are then cut by the player on the dealer's right, and the dealer distributes them face downwards one by one, beginning of course to the left.

The undealt cards must be placed in a heap face downwards in the middle of the table, and not touched until the round is over, except at Purchase Nap, when the dealer retains possession of the pack until the purchases have been effected.

The object of each player is to win as many tricks as he can. Since only five cards are dealt to each, five is obviously the highest number of tricks that can be won (or "made") in one hand.

The first move in the game is the process of "calling". The "eldest hand" (he who is seated next the dealer on the left) has the first call. He states how many tricks he thinks he can win, with all the other players against him. The rest of the players, each in his turn from left to right, now have the option of making a higher call, or of saying "pass"—which means they cannot do better than the previous caller. Thus it will be seen that the dealer always has the last call. The lowest permissible call is "two" (some players agree beforehand that it shall be "three"). The highest call, in the ordinary game, is Nap—to win all five tricks. Because this is difficult to do the player is allowed odds of two to one. That is, if he makes Nap he is paid, by each player, twice the stake for each trick. Making five counts ten. Generally it is agreed to count Nap as twelve. Thus, if the stakes are a penny a trick, the player who makes Nap gets a shilling from each of the others. If he loses he pays out sixpence each. This is the essence of the game of Nap: each player, for each hand, either "pays out" or "receives".

When everyone has called, the play begins. The highest caller has the "lead", and the first card he plays (face upwards on the table before him) *determines the "trump" suit* for the hand. (Hence it will be seen that in deciding what to call, a player is guided by the fact that he can make "trumps" the suit of which he holds the most or the strongest cards.)

The next player must, if he can, "follow suit": that is to say, he *must play a card of the same suit as the card led, if he holds one*: if not, he may discard. This rule obtains throughout all games of the Whist variety, and failure to obey it is called "revoking" and involves a severe penalty.

Similarly the other players in their turn follow suit, or discard (i.e. throw away a useless card of another suit). The player of the highest trump wins the trick. All the cards are played face upwards on the table in front of their players. When the trick is won, the winning card is turned face downwards to mark the score for the player. It will be remembered that all are playing against the caller: so it has become the custom to turn down only the caller's winning cards—since the vital point in every hand is to note whether or not the caller succeeds in his call. If he does, he receives from each of the other players one stake for each trick (except—as mentioned above, in the case of a Nap call—when he receives double stakes). It is of no advantage for him to make say five tricks if his call was "three": he receives, at penny nap, only threepence from each of his opponents. If he fails to make his three—or whatever it was—he has to pay out to each of the other players one stake per trick.

In the second and subsequent tricks, of course, the card led is not necessarily a trump, and a trick may be won by trumping: that is to say, a player having no cards of the suit led will, if he think fit, play a trump—which will beat *any* card except a higher trump.

As an illustration of the above points let us assume a game in progress, and that there are five players in this instance. Twenty-five cards will have been dealt. There are then twenty-seven, to make up the fifty-two, left in the pack. It is, therefore, just a little more than an even chance that any given card will be left in the pack and not actually dealt out. If our dealer, who has called "four" for example, has in his hand the King, Queen, ten and five of Diamonds, and the Ace of Clubs, it is about an even chance that the Ace of Diamonds will be in the pack and not dealt. As it is his own lead he plays the King of Diamonds. Diamonds then become trumps. The Ace *has* been dealt out, and the next player to the dealer puts it on the caller's King. The first trick thus goes against the caller. He has to make all the others—he is "top-weight". The winner of the first trick now plays a Heart. As the caller has no Hearts he may trump. He is now the last player, and assuming that the trick comes in to him without being trumped previously, he takes it with his five of Diamonds. He then plays again, this time the Queen of Diamonds; the Queen "draws" on this second lead of trumps, the Jack of Diamonds (i.e. one of the other players, having no other Diamond, is forced to play it: although he knows that it cannot win). The caller has now made two tricks. His ten of trumps is bound "to make" for his third trick. He has now one more trick to make, and he leads the Ace of Clubs. This card can only be beaten by a trump, but as no trumps were played to the ten which he led, he knows that he is safe. The caller has made "four", and each of the other players pays him four stakes. If there had been a small trump left in one of the hands to beat the caller's Ace of Clubs he would have "gone down", and would have had to pay each of the other players four stakes.

An absolutely sure hand at Nap is Ace, King, Queen, Jack, ten, of the same suit, as these are the highest cards in order. But Nap is often called, and made, on hands of much less value. It depends largely upon the number of players. If only three are playing there will be fifteen cards dealt, with thirty-seven remaining in the pack. It is now just about two and a half to one that a given card will be in the pack, and not dealt. On the law of averages this means that in seven hands the trump Ace or King will be in the pack five times, whilst it is only twice dealt out. *The smaller the number of players the greater will be the value of the cards that are held.* With seven players considerably more than half the cards will be dealt. It is then evident that the odds are in favour of the particular card being dealt. It would be foolish to risk a Nap with seven playing, if the King were the best card in the hand.

But when there are a number of players the caller has the advantage in the splitting up of the trumps. Let us take five players again. There are twenty-five cards dealt, rather less than one-half; there will also be, on the average, about one-half of the trump suit dealt, say six or seven at most—there being thirteen cards to the suit. If the caller has three trumps this leaves four amongst the other four players. If two are without trumps this means two each to the others. If, then, the caller can win the first two tricks, any trump will make a third trick. If the caller still has the lead an Ace is as good as a trump. From this it will be seen that a good "three" hand is Ace and King of trumps, and an Ace of another suit, or a small trump.

One kind of "four" hand has been illustrated. Another would be, say, an Ace and four other small trumps. The Ace being led would make. The second, the smallest trump, would be beaten, but it would draw the remaining trumps from the other players' hands, and the caller would make his last three tricks. It must not be understood from this that there are never three trumps out against a hand, with five players; there are sometimes even four trumps. But generally one can reckon on two trumps against the caller in any particular hand. Any four small trumps will usually make two tricks for this reason. Two leads of trumps are given and lost to the caller and the others "make". Now, as we usually expect to get only two, or at most three, trumps against a call, an Ace, King, ten, one other small trump and another Ace will usually make Nap. The Jack and Queen of trumps, if dealt to other hands, will perhaps fall to the first two tricks, and if there be a third trump against the caller, it is beaten by the ten on the third round. If the first three rounds are trumps, an Ace and a King of another suit will complete a Nap. An Ace and Queen make a good run for the double stakes, and even an Ace and Jack are always worth a run with five players.

Small cards may often, with advantage, be made trumps, and big ones of other suits used to take tricks

Thus a hand may consist of the five, seven and nine of Clubs, and two other Aces, or an Ace-King. This is a "three" hand by making the Clubs trumps. The first Club is led and lost. The next lead is up to one of the Aces. This makes. Another trump is led and lost; this clears all the trumps, leaving two winning cards in the caller's hand.

FIG. 3.—A probable "Nap" hand

If the Ace or King he holds is "led to" he wins with it and plays his trump. If anything else is led, he trumps it and plays his winning card for three.

The Ace and two of trumps, and another Ace, constitute a good "two" hand. The best play is Ace, which wins; then the second trump, which loses, and wait for the right lead. Some players think otherwise, and lead the second Ace. If this is trumped, which very often happens, there is little hope for the small trump making.

In playing *against* this call care should be used to allow as many players as possible to play after the caller. Thus, if the caller plays a small card, let this be beaten, if possible, by the player last after the caller. When he leads again the caller perhaps has to trump, and if there are three to play after him one or other of them may be able to over-trump. If the caller has only one more trick to make, lead trumps. It is then "the table" against his trump. If the caller has only a small trump left there may, by chance, be another left a little larger, which will beat it. In these circumstances, if a trick is already beaten and you hold a trump yourself, take the trick with a higher suit card, if you hold it, and lead the trump.

The foregoing gives a good idea of how orthodox Napoleon is played. There are, however, several variations of the game, to which it behoves us to pay some attention. Before doing so, however, it will perhaps be as well to set out the generally accepted rules of "Nap"; which are as follows: —

A player may call once only in each hand.

A declaration once made must stand, and cannot be altered.

A player who has trumped a suit, or discarded upon a suit before all the five tricks have been played out, and so made or defeated a declaration, must immediately show his remaining cards to prove that he has not revoked. If he should refuse to show them, he is held to have revoked, and a revoke entails the following penalties: —

On the revoke being discovered, the cards must be taken up and played properly—that is to say, players must follow suit, if they can; and always remember that a revoke is just as much a revoke if you throw away a card of another suit, holding a card of the suit led, as if you trumped under the same circumstances.

The hand having been replayed, the offender pays the stakes for himself and everyone of the other players to the caller, if the call succeeds. If the call fails, he pays the stakes to every other player, except the caller.

A revoke proved against the caller himself entails the immediate penalty of the loss of the stakes; that is to say, if a man calls three and revokes, it matters not how many tricks he makes, he must pay (at penny Nap) threepence to every one of his opponents.

If a card is exposed in the pack or in dealing, or if there is a misdeal, or if the pack is shown to be faulty, or if the cards are dealt without being cut, there should be a fresh deal by the same player.

Any player can demand a fresh deal if any one of these faults is committed, *but the demand must be made before the hands are looked at;* otherwise the deal must stand.

After all the calls have been declared, should a player discover that he has too few or too many cards the game must be played out, and if the number in the superior caller's hand be correct he takes the stakes, if he succeeds in making his call: but neither receives nor pays if he fails. Should the caller, however, hold a wrong number in his hand, he neither receives nor pays if he wins, but pays if he fails. When a Nap is declared, the game must be played out, subject to the above rules, whether the other players have their correct number or not; but, failing a Nap call, the cards must be redealt should any irregularity be discovered before all the players have declared.

On occasions when no declaration is made—i.e. when none of the players has cards sufficiently good even to call "two" or "three"—it is customary to play the next hand for double stakes. This is called a "double header", and it remains so until all is won or lost.

A player at Purchase Nap, having once bought cards or refused to buy, cannot subsequently alter his decision.

The commonest variation of Napoleon is the inclusion of the call "Wellington", which, as may be guessed, beats "Nap". Sometimes, however, it is merely called "Double Nap". The stakes won and lost are double those won and lost on a Nap call. It must be noted that Wellington cannot be called unless a previous player has called Nap.

Another additional call sometimes included is "misère"—which is really a call adapted from Solo Whist. This call ranks between "three" and "four"—but it *is paid for as a "three"*. This means *losing* all five tricks.

This variation is becoming increasingly popular, and allows the use and development of considerable skill.

Sometimes trumps are still recognised when misère is called—sometimes the hand is played without trumps. This point should be agreed in advance. If trumps are recognised, the caller should of course lead a suit of which he has but a single card.

Generally speaking, low cards are essential to a misère call. But one, or even two, quite high cards need not deter the player.

Thus a hand consisting of two of Spades, two and Ace of Diamonds, three and four of Hearts might be played as follows: lead two of Spades; this trick is practically bound to be taken by another player. The trick winner—we will suppose—leads Clubs. Having none of these, the caller can "throw away" the dangerous Ace and feel reasonably certain of losing the rest of the tricks in view of his very low cards.

If by chance the first trick winner leads Diamonds, the two can be played to lose the trick, whilst the Ace may be thrown away later. For if you have none of a particular suit, it is likely that one of your opponents will have rather more than usual of them. Hence you are fairly sure of having opportunities to throw away dangerous cards.

When playing *against* a misère call, remember that the caller's weakness, if he has any, will be in his holding two cards or more of the same suit—one perhaps fairly high. Therefore do not change the lead except for good reason. Try him again with the suit wherein he has just successfully lost a trick.

Another common practice is to allow a player who has called Nap to look at the top card on the pack—which card he may exchange for one from his hand. Sometimes it is agreed that a player must pay for this privilege by putting an agreed stake into the pool or "kitty", which is allowed to mount up until a player succeeds in getting Nap—when he takes the pool as well as his opponents' stakes.

This is called Peep Nap; and the object of both the peeping and the pool is to encourage players to take risks by calling Nap on doubtful hands, and thus increase the fun.

Another method of encouraging "sporting" calls is for every *successful* player to pay one stake into the pool. As before, the pool remains untouched until Nap is made. As successful Nap calls are sometimes very infrequent, such a pool can assume enticing proportions. In such circumstances, it is well worth risking a doubtful Nap hand to win a sum probably many times the usual amount.

Purchase Nap, which has been mentioned once or twice above, is decidedly an improvement on the ordinary game. After all the players have inspected the hands dealt to them, and before calling commences, the dealer asks each player in turn if he wishes "to buy". The player may buy any number up to five—paying one stake into the pool for *each*. In exchange for each card bought he must throw out one from his original hand, without of course showing it. These discards are not used again until the next hand. Cards cannot be exchanged more than once.

The pool goes to the first player who makes Nap.

As many more cards are "in play" for Purchase Nap than for ordinary Nap, it is necessary to restrict the number of players to not more than four; and for the reason that every player has had, practically speaking, the option of choosing his hand from ten cards, it is obvious that calls must be based on much stronger hands than in the ordinary game.

"Seven Card Nap" probably calls for more skill than any other variety. Calls may be anything up to "seven": five tricks is still called "Nap" and is paid double stakes, as usual: six tricks is paid treble stakes, and seven, usually referred to as "the lot", at quadruple stakes. The misère call is permitted and ranks next above "Nap", being paid for as a Nap.

Some players even go so far as to play "Purchase" with seven cards. A very high price, however, is put upon the fresh cards in order to discourage buying except in rare circumstances. The pool, of course, awaits the first successful caller of "the lot".

The seven card game is, however, much better when played with no "buying" and no "peep".

The following general hints may be useful to novices:

If you have won a trick against the caller do not lead trumps if he has still more than one trick to make.

If, however, he has but one more trick to make you are best advised to lead trumps if you can.

It is one of the "conventions" that when playing against an ordinary call a player's first discard should be the lowest card of his weakest suit. You should observe this convention and note what other players discard. From your observations you will be able to gather information as to what cards your "confederates" hold—and your play should be guided thereby.

But in playing against misère your first discard should be the highest card of your shortest suit—or a "singleton" unless the latter happens to be very low—a two or three. From the discard your fellow players will be guided in their leads: they will know that in that suit at any rate you can be trusted not to win the trick.

In conclusion, a novice should bear in mind that it *does matter* what he plays when he has a completely worthless hand. His apparently useless cards, used properly, in conjunction with the other players, may make all the difference between paying and receiving.

SOLO

SOLO WHIST, to give it its full name, is another member of the Whist family, and has features in common with both Napoleon and Whist proper. It stands, as it were, midway between the two.

It is played with the full pack of fifty-two cards, the values of which are as at Whist and Napoleon. Rules as to following suit and trumping are also as usual. Normally it is considered a game for four players—the whole pack being dealt in the usual way, so that each player receives thirteen cards.

It is often, however, played by three players, and sometimes by five.

When three play, the procedure is either to remove one of the suits from the pack and not use it at all, which is the simpler method; or, all the twos, threes and fours are abstracted from the pack, the players are dealt thirteen cards each, and the fortieth (last) card is turned up to indicate the trump suit, but is not used by any of the players. This latter method makes the best game. When five play each of the players in turn "stands out" for one hand, i.e. the actual play is always by four players, as in the ordinary game; but the players each play only four hands out of five.

Solo has the distinctive feature that it provides both for individual ("solo") play and partnership play. As at Nap and Whist the object of each player is to make as many tricks as he can, either by himself or in co-operation with another player.

Shuffling and cutting the pack are as at Nap: but it is the rule, or custom, to deal cards for Solo *four at a time* until the last four in the pack are reached; these are dealt singly, one to each player. (In the case of three players the deal is by threes until the last three.) The last card dealt, which normally belongs to the dealer, is turned up to indicate the trump suit.

This having been done, the eldest hand (the player on the dealer's left) has the first call. There are eight calls in Solo. They are as follows, in order of value: —

(1) A *"pass"*: meaning that the player cannot make any of the following calls.

(2) A *"proposition"*. This means that the player is prepared, with the assistance of one of the other players, to make eight tricks out of the possible thirteen, against the remaining two players in partnership.

It should be explained that once a proposition has been made any following player may, if no higher call has been made in between, "accept"; that is, signify his willingness to enter into partnership with the proposer to make between them the eight tricks.

It is more or less obvious that anyone proposing or accepting should be reasonably certain that he can make at least four tricks from his own hand.

Colloquially, "proposal" and "acceptance" are known as "prop" and "cop".

(3) *Solo*. This is the lowest "individual" call, and signifies that the caller is prepared to make five tricks, playing alone against the other players in combination.

(4) *Misère*. Meaning that the caller undertakes to *lose* every trick, the other players combining to make him win one. In the play of a misère call there are no trumps.

(5) *Abundance*. In this call the player *may make whatever suit he likes trumps*. The call signifies that he is prepared to make nine tricks, playing against the other players in combination. He must declare what suit he makes trumps before the first card is led.

(6) *Royal Abundance;* or, "abundance in trumps", is a call to make nine tricks also: but in this case the existing trump suit, as indicated by the last card dealt, stands. The call supersedes ordinary "abundance" for that reason: it cannot be made unless a previous player has called "abundance".

(7) *Open Misère*. In this call, as in misère, there are no trumps: but the player has to expose on the table the whole of his hand, *after the first trick has been*

played. It will be appreciated that the misère hand required for this call must be exceptionally strong —in view of the fact that after the first trick, the opponents have full knowledge of the caller's cards and can shape their play accordingly.

(8) *Abundance declared.* The highest call—to make all thirteen tricks. As in the ordinary abundance call, the player can make his own trumps, and plays "on his own" against the rest. In addition he has the special privilege of leading first wherever he happens to be sitting: *in all other calls the first lead is from the eldest hand, as in Whist.*

It should be noted that, contrary to the rule at Napoleon, a player at Solo may have more than one call. The eldest hand, should he happen to have "passed", may, if no higher call than a proposal has been made by the other three players, accept the proposal, when his turn comes again, if no one else has done so. No other player has this privilege.

Once a higher call is made, all previous calls are void: but a player whose call has been superseded may call again, a higher call than the last caller. The calls go round the table clockwise, until no more are forthcoming.

To illustrate this, let us take an instance; calling the players A, B, C, D—in the order they sit round the table, A being the eldest hand. Suppose A passes, B says "I propose", and C and D both pass. In this case, it is still open to A to say "I accept" if he thinks it is worth it. If he does so, A and B play as partners against C and D. They retain their places, and in playing the order is as usual, i.e. B plays *immediately after his partner* A, and D after C: contrary to the case in Whist, where the partners play alternately. Of course, if the "prop" and "cop" had been between, say, A and C, then the play would be exactly as in Whist.

Continuing our original example, if A did not choose to accept B's proposal, he would say "I pass" again, and the hand would be at an end, and a fresh deal made. Some players, however, rather than throw up the hand, play what is called "general misère". There are no trumps in this, and the object of every player is to play his cards so that he *does not take the last trick.* (The unfortunate one who does take it loses points or stakes equivalent to those for Solo.) This sounds a very simple business, but it is not.

The play is much the same as in other misère hands in that big cards are thrown away: but it is necessary to be careful in doing this, as it is often imperative to retain one or two leading cards in order to force through a suit which is dangerous to you.

Let us take another illustration. Suppose that after A has passed, B called "solo", C called "misère", and D called "abundance". A, having passed, can have no more calls: but B could, possibly, call "royal abundance" (abundance in trumps): and this in its turn might be superseded by C calling "open misère". There is still one call that D might make, to wit "abundance declared"— the highest call of all. There could be no further calling, the limit having been reached; D would proceed to play for his thirteen tricks.

At the risk of repetition, it is perhaps desirable to stress the following points: —

(a) Once having "passed", no player can call: but the eldest hand (no other player) *can* accept a proposition which is still open after the dealer has called or passed.

(b) A call having been superseded by a higher call, it no longer stands: e.g. no one can accept a proposition if a higher call has been made in the mean-while.

(c) A player who has called may, in his proper turn, increase his call to *any* higher call: e.g. having said "accepted" he may later, if he likes, call anything up to "the limit". But he *cannot* increase his call unless it has been overcalled.

The final call having been made, play proceeds as at Nap or at Whist. As mentioned above, the eldest hand always leads first, except in the case of "abundance declared" when the caller leads—after naming his trump suit. It should be noted that a player calling ordinary "abundance" or "abundance declared" does *not* name his trump suit when making his call. He waits to see whether he is over-called. If not, and his call is the highest, he names his trumps before the first card is played.

The cards are played in front of their players, and

tricks won are marked by turning face downwards the winning card. Except in the misère calls, and the highest call, it is necessary, contrary to the practice at Nap, to mark *every* trick won because it is usual to count points or stakes for what are called "undertricks" and "overtricks". This is dealt with later in connection with the scoring. The winner of each trick leads for the next; and the hand is played right out in order to ascertain the "undertricks" and "overtricks".

The maxims of good play applicable to Whist are to a large extent applicable to Solo, and a novice would do well to study these. In fact, in the case of a proposal and acceptance, where the players sit alternately—i.e. when A and C are partners against B and D—the game resolves itself for that hand into pure Whist. But when the order of the partners is otherwise—where they sit side by side— certain modifications of Whist principles are obviously necessary.

For instance, "third player play high" holds good at Whist because the third player is *always* the leader's partner. In Solo this is frequently not the case, and habitual Whist players should make a note of this, and of the fact that if you and your partner sit side by side, you should never finesse in a lead coming from him if he be sitting on your right. Also, if your partner and then an adversary have to play after you, you should win the trick with the highest of a sequence; e.g. holding King, Queen, put on the King, otherwise your partner will think the King is against you.

In propositions and acceptances trumps should be used to draw trumps in order to establish plain suits.

Never force your partner to trump if you are weak in trumps yourself.

If you have to commence the game against a misère, it is wise to lead from your shortest and weakest suit, and to lead a medium card if you have one—such as six or seven —and certainly not to commence by leading a two, unless it is a single card; and even then it is not always advisable.

Against other declarations it is well to commence with your longest suit.

Except under extreme circumstances do not lead trumps against a solo call. But if the caller refuses to lead trumps, an adversary should, if possible, put the lead with the player on the caller's right, to give him an opportunity of leading trumps through him.

As a general rule, your discards should be from your weakest and shortest suits. You should not, however, leave a King unguarded, and it is dangerous to leave a Queen only singly guarded. With a long plain suit headed by Ace, King, Queen, it is sometimes advisable to inform your partner of the fact by first discarding the Ace. In other cases, your first discard should be from your weakest suit. Subsequent discards convey no information, as they may be from strength.

Solo is usually played for money stakes. But counters can of course be used. The stakes are agreed before the game starts and the values of the various calls may be anything the players desire, being proportioned of course to the "height" of the call. The common practice is to reckon propositions and solos at six stakes, misères at twelve, and abundances at eighteen: with "open misère" as double "misère", and "abundance declared" as double "abundance." It might seem from this that calls of different value are reduced to equality, but this apparent anomaly is rectified by payment for undertricks and overtricks and by certain other factors mentioned below. (Some players, as a matter of fact, do give every call a different value, in an ascending scale from "Prop and Cop" to "Abundance declared"; and so do not reckon "unders" and "overs" at all.)

The scoring with undertricks and overtricks is as follows:—

In a proposition and acceptance, the callers each receive six stakes if they succeed (for the eight tricks) and one stake each for every trick over eight. If they do not make eight tricks they pay their opponents six stakes each for having lost the call, and in addition one stake each for every trick under eight. Thus each of them stands to win at least six stakes, but stands to lose at least seven stakes: since they can make exactly eight tricks and win the call, but cannot lose the call without paying for one "undertrick". If by good fortune they make a "grand slam", viz. all thirteen tricks, they get double stakes for the five overtricks.

It must be understood that in "prop and cop" each

player receives or pays only once, i.e., if A and C are
playing B and D, A pays B and C pays D.

In the individual calls it works out differently. In the
case of a solo a successful player receives eighteen takes
for the call (six from each opponent) with one additional stake from each opponent for every trick over five.
An unsuccessful "solo" caller would pay out six stakes
plus one stake for every undertrick to each of his
three opponents—hence his minimum gain would be
eighteen, whilst his minimum loss would be twenty-
one stakes.

There can be no overs or unders in misère—the caller
either wins or loses it. Therefore he wins or loses thirty-six
stakes, neither more nor less.

Abundance is scored similarly to solo: eighteen stakes
(per opponent) for the call, and one stake (per opponent)
for each "over" or "under". (But sometimes it is agreed
to double the "overs" but not the "unders".)

Royal abundance is paid for exactly as the preceding
call. It merely has the advantage of superseding an ordinary "abundance" call.

Open misère is paid for at double the price of misère,
and there are no "unders" or "overs". Thus the caller
stands to win or lose seventy-two stakes.

"Abundance declared" likewise is double the ordinary
call. It is lost immediately the caller loses a trick, so there
are no undertricks. The caller will either lose or win one
hundred and eight stakes, viz. at penny points, nine
shillings.

It will be seen that playing at penny points on the
above scoring (called "six, twelve, and eighteen") one is
able to lose quite a considerable sum. But stakes can of
course be smaller, say, penny, twopence, and threepence,
in place of the sixpence, shilling, and one shilling and
sixpence indicated above.

Solo has no standard code or laws, but the following
are the most important rules as generally accepted and
given by the best authorities.

The last card dealt, which indicates the trump, must
be left exposed on the table until the first trick is turned;
but the dealer may play it to the first trick, if he can
do so.

The trump indicating card having been taken up by

the dealer after the first trick, it must not be named; although anyone may ask, and must be told, what is the trump suit.

Should a card be exposed by one of the adversaries of a misère or open misère, the caller can immediately claim the stakes, and is regarded as having won the call; the stakes being paid by the offender for himself and his partners. The caller can enforce the same penalty if a card is led out of turn against him, or if a revoke is made against him, or if anyone follows suit out of turn.

An exposed card is a card that is placed face upwards on the table, or the face of which can be seen by any of the players except him to whom the card belongs. The aggrieved party can demand that the card be played or not be played, i.e. he can say, "Follow suit or play the——" (naming the exposed card), and this demand can be repeated as long as the exposed card remains unplayed. If the exposed card is a trump, and trumps are not led, the adversary may say, "Follow suit or pass the trick," when the holder of the exposed card must not trump, but must discard from another suit if he cannot follow.

An offender against this rule may throw away an exposed card if he has not a card of the led suit, or lead it when it is his turn to lead; except against a *solo* or *abundance*, when he may be prohibited from leading it. When the suit exposed is led by someone other than the offender, the adversary may say to him who exposed the card, "Play"—or "Don't play—that card"; or he can make him play either the highest or lowest of his suit.

If a player follows suit out of turn, i.e. plays before one of his partners who ought to have played before him, that partner can be compelled to play his highest or lowest of the suit, or to trump or not to trump.

If all the four players have played to the trick before any irregularity is discovered, there is no penalty except in the case of a "revoke".

No player or partnership guilty of a revoke can win a call: and every revoke entails the penalty of the loss of three tricks from the offender's score.

If, after the three tricks for a revoke are taken from the score of the offender, he still has enough tricks to win the declaration, then he simply loses the declaration, i.e. supposing a solo caller revokes, and he has made eight or nine tricks, he would, after the penalty was paid, have made enough to win the solo. He then only pays the "price of the call" to each of his opponents.

If, however, the forfeiture of the tricks brings the offender's number down below the score required by the declaration, then for each trick short the agreed price of an undertrick must also be paid.

The offending player pays the stakes in all cases of a revoke, except in the instance of a proposer and acceptor, who, being partners, pay the fine between them.

When a revoke is suspected, a player may, at the close of the hand, examine all the tricks for proof: and if the other side do not allow this examination to be properly made, the revoke is established.

Immediately after a "misère", "open misère", or "abundance declared" has been defeated the opposing players should show their hands, in order that it may be clear that no one has revoked.

There are of course many other rules, but they are of the usual nature and will be more or less understood by anyone with a little experience of games of the Whist type.

WHIST

IN past years Whist was so popular that it might almost have been described as our national card game. It has now been largely displaced by Contract Bridge, but is still popular, especially in Whist Drives.

The vast majority of people have at least some knowledge of the game, but for those who have not, a brief description must suffice.

It is played with an ordinary full pack of fifty-two cards. It is a partnership game for four players—two against two. They sit alternately at table thus:—

N

W   E

S

It has become the custom in all descriptive matter relating to Whist (and also Contract Bridge) to indicate the respective players by this lettering.

Unless otherwise agreed, the players cut for partners; those cutting the two lower cards play against those cutting the two higher. The player who cuts the lowest card of all deals. If two or more players cut equal cards, they cut again. Ace counts low in cutting.

The deal is by one card at a time to each player in turn—from left to right. Each player thus receives thirteen cards. The last card dealt (which belongs of course to the dealer's hand) is turned up to indicate the trump suit of the hand.

The object of the game is for each pair of partners to make as many tricks as possible. The player on the dealer's left (the "eldest hand") leads first. Afterwards

FIG. 4.—The "Honours" at Whist (Spades being trumps)

the winner of each trick leads. The cards are generally played to the centre of the table, one on top of another. They have their "face" values—i.e. Ace beats King, King beats Queen, and so on: "following suit", where possible, is imperative, as in Napoleon. (A novice who does not know these elementary principles should read the chapter on Napoleon.)

Whist has an elaborate code of laws—numbering a hundred or thereabout—drawn up by a committee of the foremost clubs. These deal with every possible detail of the game, and for the purposes of this book it would waste space to enumerate them all. The more important are given briefly at the end of this section. Those desiring to have the full code can obtain it from any of the well-known playing-card manufacturers.

The scoring at Whist is as follows: —

Only the tricks above six are counted. Thus—a partnership winning seven tricks out of the thirteen scores one point (the "odd trick"). Their opponents, with six tricks only, score nothing—unless "Honours" (see Fig. 4) are being played. (According to the code Honours should be scored; but most players nowadays consider that the game is better without the Honours score.) As another instance—if one side scores thirteen tricks and the other none at all, then the trick winners score seven points, and their opponents none.

Five points make a "game". Thus it will be seen that a "game" may be won in one hand, or in several. If, as instanced above, one side made seven tricks, they would win a game: but their two extra tricks over the necessary five do *not* count towards the next game.

The winners of two games out of three are said to win "the Rubber". If one side wins two games straight off, it is not necessary to play the third: a fresh rubber is commenced.

Whist is played "for love" more often than not: but where stakes are played for, it is usual to have so much on each game, and an additional stake on the rubber. Sometimes it is arranged also to have small stakes on the tricks. Thus one could have a penny or sixpence per trick, twopence or a shilling per game, and threepence or two shillings on the rubber.

All players of Whist should know what are called the "Conventions": it is surprising how many do not. The conventions are the fruit of the experience of generations of keen players: and, except for certain very rare circumstances, they are always right.

The most important are the conventional "leads".

Before giving the list of these, however, it should be remarked that the first lead (i.e. of the eldest hand) should always be "from strength": which means that the player should play one of the suit of which he has most cards.

The First Player should lead: —

Holding in plain suits (i.e. not trumps)	First time round	Second time round
Ace, King, Queen, Jack.	King.	Jack.
Ace, King, Queen.	King.	Queen.
Ace, King, and other small cards.	King.	Ace.
Ace, King only.	Ace.	King.
King, Queen, Jack with one small one.	King.	Jack.
King, Queen, Jack, and more than one other.	Jack.	King, if five, Queen if more than five.
Ace, and four or more small ones.	Ace.	Fourth best of those remaining.
King, Queen, and other small ones.	King.	If King wins, fourth best of those remaining.
Ace, Queen, Jack, with or without one small one.	Ace.	Queen.
Ace, Queen, Jack with two or more small ones.	Ace.	Jack.
King, Jack, ten, nine.	Nine.	King, if Ace or Queen falls to the first lead.
King, Jack, ten.	Ten.	
Queen, Jack, ten, nine.	Queen.	Nine.
Queen, Jack and one small one.	Queen.	
Queen, Jack, and two or more small ones.	Fourth best.	

Holding, in trumps:—

Ace, King, Queen, Jack.	Jack.	Queen.
Ace, King, Queen.	Queen.	King.
Ace, King, and five other small ones.	King.	Ace.
Ace, King, and fewer than five small ones.	Fourth best.	

The above combinations do not of course illustrate every possible hand. Where you hold combinations differing from the above, the convention is that you should lead the *fourth best card of your longest suit*.

The value of these leads lies in the fact that they assist you to ascertain who holds the cards which you do not hold: and at the same time give some indication to your partner as to what cards you yourself hold, so that he may shape his play accordingly.

The reasons for playing in the way indicated are not far to seek in the majority of the cases, and will become self-evident to a novice ere he has been playing long. Some examples are given later.

The conventions for the leader's partner (that is, the third player) come next in importance. Probably the one convention that *is* thoroughly well known in Whist is "third player, play high." But there is more than this. Quite probably the third player holds cards of equal value (equal value, that is to say, as regards taking a particular trick). He may hold, for instance, Ace, King, and Queen, or Queen, Jack, and ten. Any one of the three is as good as another so far as taking the trick is concerned. When such is the case, the third player should *not* play the highest, but the lowest of the three. This convention is very important and is usually phrased, "Win with smallest and return highest." Thus, if he holds King, Queen, and Jack of the suit led, he will play the Jack. If it wins he will "return his partner's lead" (another important convention) by leading the King. If it loses, he will lead the King as soon as he has an opportunity. His partner will, after the two tricks have been played, know exactly where the Queen is.

The conventional, and therefore the wisest, play for the third player, may be summarised as follows: —

The Third Player plays his best card except when: —
(1) the second player plays a card higher than any card held by the third hand; the lowest card is then played;
(2) a sequence is held, such as King, Queen, Jack; Queen, Jack; Ace, King, etc.; then play the lowest or lower card of the sequence;
(3) a "finesse" is obligatory or desirable.

It is necessary here to explain what is meant by a

"finesse": it is the winning of a trick by an inferior card when another, better, perhaps the top card, is in hand. As an example: if your partner leads Diamonds from two cards, an eight and four, and you as third player have Ace, Queen, seven and six, you would finesse the Queen if you played it on the first round and the second player held the King. This appears to be against the rule, "third player play high." But you must be governed always by the exact cards you hold. In this case you would return your partner's lead with the Ace, and then give him a small Diamond on the third round so that he could trump.

Finesses are of two kinds, speculative and obligatory.

The finesse speculative is as follows: you hold Ace, Queen; or Ace, Queen, Jack of a suit, which your partner leads. You play the Queen, if you hold Ace, Queen; or Jack if you hold Ace, Queen, Jack. This play is adopted on the chance that the King is to your right and is therefore a "speculation".

The finesse obligatory is as follows: you hold King, ten, seven, and three of a suit, and you lead the three; your partner plays the Queen, and wins the trick, and returns a small card of the suit. From the fact of the Queen winning, you know the Ace is not held by your right-hand adversary; you also know your partner does not hold the Jack. When your partner returns a small card of the suit, you know he does not hold the Ace. If both the Ace and Jack are to your left, it matters not whether you play King or ten. If, however, the Jack be to your right, your ten draws the Ace, and you remain with the King, the best card of the suit. Hence you are *obliged* to play the ten as third player in order to give yourself one chance —viz., that the Jack is to your right; consequently, this is called the finesse obligatory.

In returning his partner's lead, the third player should (1) play his highest card if he held, originally, three cards of the suit; and (2) play his lowest card if he held, originally, more than three of the suit.

So far we have dealt only with the play of the leader and his partner. We must now turn our attention to their opponents. The conventional and wisest play on their part for the special circumstances is given in the subjoined list; but it will be realised, of course, that all conceivable situations cannot be provided for. The second player must

B

often be guided solely by circumstances. In fact, the second player has less to guide him in the form of conventions than any other player; and it is in his play as "second in hand" that the really good Whist player shows his calibre.

The Second Player:—

When the card led is:—	and holding:—	should play:—
A small one.	Ace, King, Queen.	The Queen.
A small one.	Ace, King, Jack.	The King.
A small one.	Ace, King, and other small ones.	The King.
A small one.	Ace, Queen, ten, and others.	The Queen.
A Jack.	Ace, Queen, ten, and others.	The Ace.
A small trump.	Ace, Queen, ten, and others.	The ten.
A small one.	Ace, Queen, and small ones.	A small one.
A small one.	Ace, Jack, ten, and others.	A small one.
A small trump.	Ace, Jack, ten, and others.	The ten.
A small one.	Ace, and small one.	A small one.
A small one.	King, Queen, Jack, and others.	The Jack.
A small one.	King, Queen, and others.	The Queen.
A small one.	Queen, Jack, ten, and others.	The ten.
A small one.	Queen, Jack, and small ones.	The Jack.
A Queen.	Ace, and small one.	The Ace.
A Queen.	King, and other small ones.	A small one.
A small one.	King, and one small one.	A small one.
A small one.	Queen, and one small one.	A small one.
A Jack or ten.	Queen, and one small one.	The Queen.

Note: A "small" card, generally speaking, means a nine or under.

It will be observed that sometimes in similar circumstances, the play in the case of trumps is different from that in the case of plain suits. This is for the very good reason that trumps cannot be trumped, whereas plain suits may be.

The general objects of the second player may be summarised as (1) to protect his partner, and (2) to give his partner as much information as possible as to what cards of the suit in play remain in his (the second player's) hand.

The Fourth Player has to take the trick if he can. He should take it with the lowest card possible. If he cannot take it, he "discards"—according to the conventions that are given below.

Nothing but brains and experience will make an expert Whist player; but the following general principles will be useful to beginners (and to *some* "old hands" as well!).

The maxim that the third player should return his partner's lead does not mean that he must return it at once, nor at the very next opportunity. An immediate return of your partner's suit is generally taken to mean either that you have no more of that suit, and can trump on the third round; or that you have an extremely weak hand and can commence no sort of offensive yourself.

As a general rule, if you have some good cards of another suit, you should lead that suit, finding out, incidentally, how your partner stands in that direction, and establish the suit if he can assist to the normal degree. Then when this is done, return your partner's lead.

"Throwing away" or discarding is usually looked upon as a simple matter of no importance. This is not so. One of the main objects in Whist play is to give your partner as much information as possible regarding the cards you hold; this can be done when discarding as well as when winning or attempting to win tricks.

When discarding, adhere to the following three minor conventions:—

(1) If trumps have *not* been led, nor "called for" by either of your opponents—discard the lowest of your *weakest* suit.

(2) If your opponents *have* led trumps, or either of them has called for trumps—discard the lowest of your *strongest* suit.

(3) If your partner has led trumps, and you have no trumps—discard the lowest of your weakest suit.

It should be remembered, however, with regard to (2) that if you have previously had the lead, and thereby indicated to your partner which is your strongest suit, there is no necessity to throw away one of that suit; and you may discard, as usual, your most worthless card.

Whilst on the subject of conveying information to your partner it may be remarked that, of course, your opponents will be, or should be, able to interpret your play as easily as your partner (except for the fact that they cannot know as thoroughly as he does what is in *his* hand). Hence it sometimes pays to play *incorrectly*. This is called "false carding". It is, however, a refinement that should be attempted only in desperate circumstances, and by players who know well what they are doing: and it must be remembered that your partner as well as your opponents will be deceived.

Mention was made on p. 35 of "calling for" trumps. This is done by playing *an unnecessarily high card* to a trick. For instance, a third player who takes a trick with an Ace, "returns" the King and then plays a small card, would be considered as having called for trumps by playing the Ace, which was unnecessarily high: his partner should lead trumps to him in due course. Again, supposing a second or fourth player plays, say, a six the first time a suit is led; and on the second round plays a lower card, say, a four—then it is obvious that he must have some reason for doing so. His reason is that he wishes his partner to lead trumps.

Trumps should not be called for rashly. Four trumps, including two honours, *plus* medium strength in one or two other suits, is the *minimum* hand on which a call for trumps should be made.

Care must be taken when observing the discards of your partner; you should be quite sure that a card *was* unnecessarily high before you answer what you think is a "call".

In answer to a call for trumps, a player should play the Ace, if he has it, at the first opportunity. Failing the Ace, he should play the highest of three trumps, or the lowest of four or more.

Trumps should be *led* as soon as possible when five or more are held. Of course, if it is seen that the strong trumps lie with the opposing partners, the trump lead should not be continued; and the player must use his trumps as best he can in other ways.

Again, should it be observed that an adversary is calling for trumps, then a player with five trumps would not lead them; but except in these circumstances it is rarely wise not to do as the convention directs.

As regard trumping his opponent's plain suits, the player must use his judgment. If he is very strong in trumps he may consider that more tricks will result in the long run if he reserves his trumps until trumps are led. In such a case he would discard and let an opponent have the trick: and his partner would consider this as a strong call for trumps, and lead them accordingly.

One serious fault which the beginner at Whist should learn to avoid is the unnecessary or too frequent changing of the suit. If you have led a certain suit and find that your opponents hold the best cards in that suit, it is *not* absolutely necessary to switch over to some other suit. If your opponents hold the best cards of the suit, they will probably "make" them sooner or later; and it is often the wisest play to lead a third round of that suit, rather than change, for the reason that this will place the lead with one of your opponents. When one of your opponents leads either you or your partner will be the last player: and the last player has an advantage over the other players, particularly towards the end of a game.

"Placing the lead" is an important item in good Whist play. It is an art that cannot be mastered in five minutes; but its advantages are easily perceived in a situation where you hold, say, Ace and Queen in one or more suits. Holding such cards it will be immensely to your advantage to be last player, for then you will be able to win with both Ace and Queen: i.e., if the King is played by either of your opponents you will beat it with the Ace, and win the next trick with the Queen.

In any position save that of last player you would run the risk of failing to "make" your Queen, and of "drawing" the King uselessly from your partner (should he hold it unguarded) when playing your Ace.

A "thirteenth card" (i.e. the last card of a suit, all the others having been played in previous tricks) is very frequently played in an attempt to place the lead. In fact, such a card should never be led except for this purpose. Your partner has to use his judgment as to where it is you are trying to place the lead. If he thinks it is with himself, he will play his biggest trump in an attempt to win the trick: or he will pass the trick (by discarding), leaving the lead with the opponent on his right or left as the case may be.

Games of Whist are usually won or lost by the play in the last four or five tricks of the hands, and it is in this phase of the hand that skill manifests itself. When this point is reached, the player should have a fairly accurate idea as to who holds the remaining cards of each suit. He can have no such knowledge of course unless he has noted who has played what, and can remember exactly which cards of every suit *have* been played.

It is surprising how many players one meets who say they "never can remember": these ought to give up playing Whist.

A beginner with a reasonably good memory should have no difficulty in quickly becoming a capable player, provided he masters the conventions and maxims that have been given: the following examples of correct play, according to conventions, may help in removing his initial difficulties.

Suppose, for instance, that your partner leads a King. You have not the Ace, and the question arises, where is it? Suppose, further, that the second player plays a small card and the fourth player wins the trick with a trump.

The Ace is obviously held by your partner. For, if the second player had held it he would have taken the trick with it, thinking that if he did not the King would win. Similarly, the fourth player could not have played a trump if he could have taken the trick with the Ace.

Again, suppose your partner leads an Ace; and that the play is as before, the trick being trumped by the fourth player. In this case you can definitely place the King with the second player, because your partner would have played it had he held both Ace and King; you have not got it, and the fourth player could not have trumped if *he* held it.

As another example, take the following: —

Suppose you hold four Hearts: the Ace, Queen, five, and two. Your partner, we will say, leads the seven of that suit as his first lead. From this you will conclude that Hearts are his strong suit. The second player plays, say, the three. You, according to convention, play the Queen, and the last player plays, perhaps, the six.

Having won the trick, you return your partner's lead by playing the Ace of Hearts. The player on your left plays the eight, your partner plays the four, and your other opponent, as fourth player, plays the ten.

You have now won two tricks in Hearts and have the next lead. What are you to do?

If you have watched carefully you will know the following. Your partner having led the seven, and played the four to your Ace, which was reasonably certain to win the trick—it is safe to assume that he led, correctly, with his "fourth best" out of five Hearts. Hence he has three more Hearts. Now you yourself have still two more, making five still unplayed: and since eight have been played in the two tricks, making the whole thirteen, it is obvious that your opponents have no more Hearts at all. Further, you will know that the Hearts your partner holds are the nine, Jack, and King—since you still hold five and two, and the seven, three, Queen, six, Ace, eight, four and ten have been played.

Your partner will also know, by a similar train of reasoning, that you hold the five and two, and the opponents none.

The correct play for both of you in these circumstances is not to lead Hearts again until trumps have been played, except, perhaps, for the purpose of "drawing" big trumps.

As a final instance, imagine that you have first lead and that you hold Queen, nine, eight, six, and two. Your correct lead is six—fourth best. Suppose the second player plays the seven and your partner wins the trick with the Ace, whilst the last player plays the five. Your partner returns your lead with the three. Your right hand opponent, the second player, plays the King on this, and since you cannot beat the King you play your lowest—the two; and the fourth player will also play a low card—say, the four.

From this play your partner should know that you have three more of this suit since you have played the two on a lost trick after leading with the six—obviously your "fourth best" of five. You, also, should know that he has no more of that suit. The Jack and ten are the only cards you have not seen, and had your partner held either or both of them, he would have returned your lead with one of them, in accordance with the convention.

Hence you know that you are in a position to lead the suit again, at a suitable opportunity, with a fair prospect of making a trick or two. Your Queen is the best remaining card, and your partner is ready to trump the suit.

The following are the more important laws of Whist:
The deal commences with the player who cuts the

original lowest card, the next deal falls to the player on his left, and so on until the rubber is finished.

There must be a new deal by the same dealer: —

(1) If, during a deal, or during the play of a hand, the pack be proved incorrect or imperfect.

(2) If any card, excepting the last, be faced in the pack.

(3) If a player takes up another player's hand.

It is a misdeal: —

(1) Unless the cards are dealt into four packets, one at a time in regular rotation, beginning with the player to the dealer's left.

(2) Should the dealer place the last (which is called the trump) card, face downwards, on his own or on any other packet.

(3) Should the trump card not come in its regular order to the dealer; but he does not lose his deal if the pack be proved imperfect.

(4) Should a player have fourteen or more cards, and any of the other three less than thirteen, unless the excess has arisen through the act of an adversary, in which case there must be a fresh deal.

(5) Should the dealer touch, for the purpose of counting, the cards on the table or the remainder of the pack.

(6) Should the dealer deal two cards at once, or two cards to the same hand, and then deal a third; but if, prior to dealing the third card, the dealer can, by altering the position of one card only, rectify such error, he may do so, except as provided by the second paragraph of this law.

(7) Should the dealer omit to have the pack cut to him, and the adversaries discover the error, prior to the trump card being turned up, and before looking at their cards, but not after having done so.

A misdeal loses the deal unless, during the dealing, either of the adversaries touch the cards prior to the dealer's partner having done so; but should the latter have first interfered with the cards, notwithstanding either or both of the adversaries having subsequently done the same, the deal is lost.

The dealer, when it is his turn to play to the first trick, should take the trump card into his hand.

After the dealer has taken up the trump card, it must not be asked for. A player who "names" it during the band is liable to have his highest or lowest trump "called". Any player may inquire, and be told, at any time what suit is trumps.

Note: "Calling" a card or suit is demanding that it shall be played. This penalty may be exacted against an offender in various circumstances, and he *must* play the card or suit "called" if he holds it.

Honours, i.e. Ace, King, Queen, and Jack of trumps are thus reckoned: —

If a player and his partner, either separately or conjointly, hold: —

(1) The four honours, they score four points.

(2) Any three honours, they score two points.

Those players who, at the commencement of a deal, are at the score of four, cannot score honours.

The penalty for a revoke takes precedence of all other scores. Tricks score next. Honours last.

Honours, unless claimed before the trump card of the following deal is turned up, cannot be scored.

To score honours is not sufficient; they must be claimed at the end of the hand: if so claimed, they may be scored at any time during the game. If the tricks won, added to honours held, suffice to make game, it is sufficient to call game.

The following are "exposed" cards: —

(1) Two or more cards played at once, face upwards.

(2) Any card dropped with its face upwards, in any way on or above the table, even though snatched up so quickly that no one can name it.

(3) Every card named by the player holding it.

All exposed cards are liable to be called, and must be left or placed face upwards on the table. If two or more cards are played at once, the adversaries have a right to call which they please to the trick in course of play, and afterwards to call the remainder. A card is not an exposed card, under the preceding law, when dropped on the floor, or elsewhere below the table. An adversary may not require any exposed card to be played before it is the turn of the owner of the card to play; should he do so, he loses his right to exact the penalty for that trick.

If a card be detached from the rest of the hand, which

an adversary at once correctly names, such card becomes an exposed card; but should the adversary name a wrong card, he is liable to have a suit called when he or his partner next have the lead.

If any player lead out of turn, his adversaries may either call the card erroneously led, or may call a suit from him or his partner when it is next the turn of either of them to lead. The penalty of calling a suit must be exacted from whichever of them next obtains the lead. It follows that if the player who leads out of turn is the partner of the person who ought to have led, and a suit is called, it must be called at once from the right leader. If he is allowed to play as he pleases, the only penalty that remains is to call the card erroneously led. The fact that the card erroneously led has been played without having been called, does not deprive the adversaries of their right to call a suit. If a suit is called, the card erroneously led may be replaced in the owner's hand.

If it is one player's lead, and he and his partner lead simultaneously, the penalty of calling the highest or lowest card of the suit properly led may be exacted from the player in error, or the card simultaneously led may be treated as a card liable to be called.

It is a revoke when a player, holding one or more cards of the suit led, plays a card of a different suit. The penalty for a revoke:—

(1) Is at the option of the adversaries, who, at the end of the hand, may either take three tricks from the revoking player, and add them to their own tricks, or deduct three points from his score, or add three to their own score (the adversaries may consult as to which penalty they will exact).

(2) Can be claimed for as many revokes as occur during the hand, and a different penalty may be exacted for each revoke.

(3) Is applicable only to the score of the game in which it occurs.

(4) Cannot be divided, i.e. a player cannot add one or two to his own score and deduct one or two from the revoking player.

(5) Takes precedence of every other score, e.g. the claimants two, their opponents nothing. The former add three to their score, and thereby win

the game, even should the latter have made thirteen tricks, and held four honours.

If a player who has become liable to have the highest
or lowest of a suit called, or to win or not to win a trick
(when able to do so) fails to play as desired, or if a player,
when called on to lead one suit, leads another, having in
his hand one or more cards of that suit demanded, he
incurs the penalty of a revoke.

At the end of a hand, the claimants of a revoke may
search all the tricks.

If a player discovers his own revoke, directly it is made.
the adversaries, whenever they think fit, may call the card
thus played in error, or may require him to play his highest
or lowest card to that trick in which he has renounced
—any player or players who have played after him may
withdraw their cards and substitute others; the cards
withdrawn are not liable to be called.

If a revoke be claimed, and the accused player or his
partner, after such claim has been made, mix the cards
before they have been sufficiently examined by the adversaries, the revoke is established. Prior to such claim, the
mixing of the cards renders the proof of a revoke difficult,
but does not prevent the claim, and possible establish-
ment of the penalty.

A revoke cannot be claimed after the cards have been
duly cut for the following deal.

The revoking player and his partner may, under all
circumstances, require the hand in which the revoke has
been detected to be played out.

SCOTCH WHIST

THIS game is called "Catch the Ten".

Thirty-six cards only are used—all below the six being
excluded. The cards rank as at Whist, except in the case
of the trump suit, in which, for the time being, the Jack
is made the best card, other cards ranking as usual.

The normal number of players is four, but any number
from two to seven may play. When the number of players
is odd, the six of Spades is also removed from the pack.
When four play, they play as partners.

Two, three, five or seven play "cut-throat", i.e. each against the rest. Six may play three against three (sitting alternately) or in three pairs (also sitting alternately), each pair against the other two pairs.

When two or three play, the cards are dealt in hands of six. Two players have three hands each, three players have two hands each. These hands are played independently.

When more play, the cards are dealt in the usual way, an equal number to each player.

The last card dealt is turned up as trumps.

Fig. 5.—The order of the high trumps
at Scotch Whist

The distinctive feature of the game is that certain of the cards have special scoring values, and it is the object of the players to win the particular tricks which contain these cards.

They are:—

Jack of trumps, which counts	11	points.
Ten	,,	,,	,,	10	,,
Ace	,,	,,	,,	4	,,
King	,,	,,	,,	3	,,
Queen	,,	,,	,,	2	,,

The game proceeds as at ordinary Whist as regards following suit, revoking, etc. The penalty exacted for a revoke varies. It should be agreed upon beforehand.

The first player, or partnership, to score forty-one points wins the game. There are no rubbers. At the end of the hand the players each count the cards in the tricks they have taken, and each scores an additional point per card above the number he started with (i.e. the number dealt to him). It will be seen that the eleven points for the Jack of trumps are bound to go to him who receives it in the deal; since it is the highest card in the pack. But the ten points carried by the ten of trumps must be played for: because Ace, King, and Queen of trumps will beat the ten in a trick although their *scoring* value is lower. The great point of the game is to "catch the ten"—because it makes a difference of twenty points, i.e. ten more for you and ten less for your opponents, or vice versa.

GERMAN WHIST

THIS is a form of Whist for two players only.

A full pack of fifty-two cards is used.

After dealing himself and his opponent the usual Whist hands of thirteen cards the dealer turns up the twenty-seventh card to indicate the trump suit, and places it on top of the remainder of the pack, which is laid face downwards in the centre of the table.

The object of each player is to make tricks in the usual way—rules as to following suit, trumping, revoking, etc., being as at Whist. Each hand constitutes a game—the winner being he who makes most tricks. A draw is possible by each getting thirteen tricks.

The non-dealer has the lead. The winner of the first trick takes the top (trump) card off the pack and the loser takes the next (which is not exposed, and which he does not show). A fresh card is turned up on top of the pack (this does not alter the trump suit) and the next trick proceeds in the same way. It will be seen that the winner of each trick gets a card which his opponent has seen, whilst the loser gets one that his opponent has not seen.

When all the cards in the pack have been drawn the hand is played out in the usual way. At this stage each player, if he has watched the cards, should know exactly what cards his opponent holds.

In view of this fact, a player should always endeavour to obtain the lead to the fourteenth trick. Then, if he holds the right cards, he could "draw" his opponent's trumps, and then make all his tricks in plain suits. If he cannot do this he should play a losing card and give his opponent the lead—on the off-chance that the latter will make a miscalculation and allow him to gain an additional trick or two by trumping.

DUMMY WHIST

DUMMY is an adaptation of Whist, for three players. Four hands are dealt, and one is exposed on the table, and is called "Dummy". The rules of the game are exactly similar to those of Whist, except that "Dummy" cannot revoke—since his cards are all exposed and any player may speak to prevent an accidental revoke.

The game may be played as "Cut-throat Dummy", in which each player in turn has Dummy as partner and keeps his own score. Or one player may elect to take Dummy as a permanent partner.

If Dummy's partner leads from his own hand when he should have led from Dummy, or vice versa, the opponents may "call a suit" from the hand which properly should have led. Dummy's partner is not liable to any penalty for an offence which does his opponents no harm (e.g. such as exposing his own cards).

The play of the hand at Dummy Whist is on the same principles as that in Bridge, except that considerations of score do not enter.

BRIDGE

WHEN most people speak of Bridge, they mean Contract Bridge; for Bridge itself is hardly played at all nowadays. For this reason the game will not be described in detail; but a few words may be said about it to show how Contract evolved out of Whist.

The old game of Bridge differs from Whist mainly in the way the trump suit is selected. In Whist trumps are chosen by the luck of the deal; in Bridge the trump suit is named by either the dealer or his partner.

Secondly, in Bridge the cards of the dealer's partner

THE BEST CARD GAMES

are laid exposed on the table, and the dealer plays them as well as his own hand; his partner takes no part in the play of the hand.

Thirdly, the suits have a different value, and points are scored for Honours ("above the line") and Tricks ("below the line"). It is interesting to note that the order of suit ranking in Bridge, from low to high, is Spades, Clubs, Diamonds, Hearts.

AUCTION BRIDGE

BRIDGE was eventually superseded by Auction Bridge, which for many years was tremendously popular. It has now been superseded by Contract Bridge, and will therefore not be described in detail here.

The main difference between Auction and the older game of Bridge is in the choice of the trump suit. The declaration, instead of being made by the dealer or his partner, is put up to "auction", each player bidding in his turn. The highest bid becomes the "final declaration" on which the hand is played; and the player who first named the trump suit (or "no trumps") of the final declaration which he or his partner has made, plays the hand, his partner becoming dummy.

The scoring resembles that used in Bridge, but when a declaration is not made, the opponents score only "above the line". These terms "above the line" and "below the line" will be explained in the article on Contract Bridge; the important thing to note here is that in Auction Bridge the scoring is less favourable to defensive play than in Bridge itself. In Contract Bridge it is still less favourable.

Another point of difference is that the suit values run (from low to high): Clubs, Diamonds, Hearts, Spades.

The general principles of bidding and play in Auction Bridge are very similar to those in Contract, and anyone who knows the latter game can master Auction in a very short time. The essential difference is that only those tricks actually contracted for can score towards game in Contract, whereas in Auction all tricks made score towards game. There is thus no incentive in Auction to bid any higher than is necessary to outbid the opponents; in Contract, as will be seen, it is quite different.

CONTRACT BRIDGE

CONTRACT BRIDGE is now firmly established as the most popular partnership card game in the world. It developed out of Auction, and at one time players learnt Auction first and then went on to Contract. Nowadays, with so many old Auction players having gone over to Contract, it is usual to learn Contract from the beginning.

Like Whist, Contract Bridge is played by four players, each pair being a partnership. Partners are arranged either by general agreement beforehand or by drawing, and the draw also determines the first dealer. The procedure for the draw is described on page 9.

The deal is made as in Whist, and as soon as it is completed the bidding starts. A bid is a declaration to make a certain number of tricks above six with a particular suit as trumps, or with no trumps. Thus when a player bids "one club", he is contracting to make, with his partner's hand, seven tricks with clubs as trumps. If he bids "three no-trumps" he is contracting to make nine tricks without any trump suit.

Bidding is competitive, and each fresh bid must be higher than the last one. The value of a bid depends firstly on the number of tricks contracted for, and secondly on the ranking of the suit chosen as trumps. No-trumps rank the highest; then come spades, hearts, diamonds, and clubs, in that order (from highest to lowest). So "one heart" is a higher bid than "one diamond"; "one no-trump" is higher than "one heart"; but a bid of "two clubs" is higher than any bid at the "one" level, including "one no-trump". "One club" is the lowest bid that can be made; the highest is "seven no-trumps", which means that the bidder is contracting to make all thirteen tricks when the hand is played without trumps.

Players bid in turn in the order of the deal. The dealer has the privilege of making the first bid, and he is followed by the player on his left. Each player must either bid, double, redouble, or pass (saying "no bid"). The bidding ends when there are three passes in succession, and the last bid made becomes the contract. If, however, all four players pass at the start, the hand is thrown in and the next deal begins.

A player may double an opponent's bid or redouble an opponent's double only provided that no other bid has intervened. All doubles and redoubles are nullified by any subsequent bid.

There are various penalties for improper bids which would require too much space to be fully described here. Details of these and of other irregularities will be found in "The International Laws of Contract Bridge" promulgated by the Portland Club and published by De La Rue Stationers Ltd. Some of the irregularities and penalties are similar in principle to those already described in the section on Whist, but differences of application are considerable.

The player who for his side bids the suit named in the final contract becomes the declarer, and plays his partner's hand as well as his own, the partner becoming dummy. Thus the player who makes the last bid does not necessarily play the hand; if, for example, he calls "four spades", and "one spade" was previously called by his partner, the latter becomes the declarer and plays the hand.

The first lead is made by the player on the left of the declarer. As soon as he has led a card, dummy spreads his hand in front of him, face up, arranged in suits. The game now proceeds, with the declarer playing the exposed hand as well as his own, and with dummy taking no further part in the game.

The playing of the cards is exactly the same as in Whist, except that if the game is played in no trumps, a player who cannot follow suit has no option but to "throw away" or discard.

The scoring, however, is completely different. The scoring in Contract Bridge is not really difficult, and it can be quickly mastered. It is most important that it should be, and that each player should keep a score—not merely as a record of the game, but for his own guidance during the game. It is absolutely essential that every player should understand the principles of scoring, as bidding must be based entirely on these.

The score is entered on a tablet or sheet of paper ruled into vertical columns, which are usually headed

"We" and "They" respectively. Half-way down the scoring sheet a horizontal line is drawn right across the columns; and it is on this line that the terms "above the line" and "below the line" are based. Each side has a "trick score" and a "premium score"; premium points are all marked above the line, and the trick score is marked below.

The score is computed according to the table on the next page, which needs some explanation for beginners.

The first of the three panels on this table concerns trick points, which are gained only by the declarer who succeeds in making his contract. No trick points are gained by him if he fails to make his contract, and trick points cannot be scored by the defenders in any circumstances.

"Odd tricks" means the number of tricks made over six; that is, the number named in the bid. So if the contract is two spades, and eight tricks are made, the declarer gains 2 x 30 = 60 trick points, and these are entered below the line. If this contract was doubled by an opponent, 120 points are scored; if it was redoubled, 240 points. It will be seen from the table that a successful contract of one no-trump gains 40 points, but two no-trumps gains 70, three no-trumps gains 100, and so on.

Only the odd tricks *bid and won* are scored as trick points. If the bid is two spades, and the declarer makes five spades (i.e. eleven tricks), he still gets only 60 points below the line. The three odd tricks made over his contract count as overtricks, and are scored above the line.

The second and third panels on the scoring table relate entirely to premium points, all of which are scored above the line. It will be seen that if the contract is undoubled, overtricks obtain the normal trick value; so in the case just mentioned, where there were three overtricks with spades as trumps, 90 points are scored above the line. Increased points are awarded where the contract is doubled or redoubled, and the figure depends on whether or not the declarer's side is "vulnerable". The meaning of this term will be explained shortly. Also, there is an additional bonus of 50 points for a side making a doubled or redoubled contract.

"Undertricks" can be scored only by defenders, and these points are gained when the declarer fails to make

CONTRACT BRIDGE SCORING TABLE

	Odd Tricks Bid and Won in	Undoubled	Doubled
Trick Points For Contractor	Clubs or Diamonds, each	20	40
	Hearts or Spades, each	30	60
	No-Trump { first each	40	80
	subsequent	30	60

Redoubling doubles the doubled points for Odd Tricks.
Vulnerability does not affect points for Odd Tricks.
100 Trick Points constitute a Game.

	Overtricks	Not Vulnerable	Vulnerable
Premium Points for Defenders — Contractors	Undoubled, each	Trick Value	Trick Value
	Doubled, each	100	200
	Making Doubled or Redoubled Contract	50	50
	Undertricks		
	Undoubled, each	50	100
	Doubled { first each	100	200
	subsequent	200	300

Redoubling doubles the doubled points for Overtricks and Undertricks, but does not affect the points for making Doubled Contracts.

Premium Points for Contractors—Holders	**Honours in One Hand** { All Honours	150
	Four Trump Honours	100
	Slams Bid and Won { Little, not vulnerable 500, vulnerable	750
	Grand „ „ 1000, „	1500
	Rubber Points { Two game	700
	Three game	500

Unfinished Rubber—The Winners of one game score 300 points. If but one side has a part score in an unfinished game, it scores 50 points.
Doubling and Redoubling do not affect points for Honours, Slams, or Rubber.
Vulnerability does not affect points for Honours.

his contract. The number of undertricks is the number of tricks by which the declarer falls short of his contract; so if the contract is three diamonds, and he makes only seven tricks, his opponents score points for two undertricks, and these are marked above the line in their column. The number of points awarded for undertricks depends upon whether the contract is doubled or redoubled and whether the declarer is vulnerable.

Finally, the third panel on the scoring sheet gives details of special bonuses. The Honour cards in Bridge are the same as in Whist—Ace, King, Queen, Jack, and Ten of the trump suit. Points for Honours are scored only if four or five are held in one hand. There are no points for Honours shared between partners. When a hand is played in no-trumps the Honour cards are the four aces, which score 150 points. Honours can be scored by defenders as well as contractors.

FIG. 6.—The "Honours" at Bridge (Clubs)

FIG. 7.—The "Honours" at Bridge where there are no trumps

Then there are the special bonuses for slams. A Little Slam, or Small Slam, consists of twelve tricks bid and won; a Grand Slam is thirteen tricks bid and won. Slam bonuses are in addition to the normal trick points and any other bonuses awarded (e.g., overtrick, Honours, etc.). Bonuses for either slam are gained only if the contract is bid as well as won. If the call is five spades, and twelve tricks are made, there is no slam bonus. If the call is six spades, and thirteen tricks are made, the bonus is for a Little Slam, not a Grand Slam. If the call is seven spades, and twelve tricks are made, no slam bonus of any sort is awarded.

The last bonus is for making the rubber, and it will be seen that it is higher if the rubber is finished in two games than it is when it takes three. A rubber consists of the best of three "games".

A "game" in Contract Bridge is scored when either side scores 100 points *below the line*. It may be won in a single hand—for example, with a successful contract of three no-trumps (100 points), four hearts or spades (120 points), or five clubs or diamonds (100 points); or with a doubled contract such as two spades ($2 \times 60 = 120$ points); or with a redoubled contract such as one spade ($4 \times 30 = 120$ points). Alternatively, a game may be won in two or more hands. It may be won, for example, by successful contracts of one heart (30 points), two diamonds (40 points), and one no-trump (40 points).

As soon as either side gains 100 or more points below the line, a line is drawn under all the trick points scored so far by either side. A game has been won, and the next game in the rubber now begins, with each side starting from zero below the line. So if one side scores 40 trick points, and then the other side scores 100 trick points, the 40 points do not count as a start towards the next game.

There is no bonus for making game, but it is obviously of great value since it is the first step towards gaining the rubber. When a side makes game it becomes "vulnerable". This has no effect on the procedure for bidding or play, but affects the scoring. As will be seen from the table, some bonuses are higher for a vulnerable side, and all penalties scored against them are higher.

When the rubber is finished the score is added up, and

for this purpose the "line" is ignored and points above and below are treated equally.

The great popularity of Contract Bridge is due to the fact that it is primarily a game of skill. Of course there is luck in it, according to the deal; but in the long run, when the luck evens out, it is invariably the more skilful players who win.

While the playing of the hand calls for skill, it may be said that the game is won or lost mainly in the bidding. The reward at Contract is not for the number of tricks won, but for the number of tricks *bid and won*. These are the only tricks that gain points below the line, and it is only points scored below the line that gain the big bonuses for rubber and slam.

For this reason bidding must not be timid. It must not be rash, of course, for the penalties are severe; but it should be up to the strength of the cards received. If a side makes a habit of calling four spades and winning only seven tricks, that is bad bidding, but if a side makes a habit of calling one spade and winning ten tricks, that is equally bad bidding! When a side is dealt good cards it must make the best possible contract out of them, or it can never hope to win.

The first thing to consider in bidding is the position of the game. If you are vulnerable, bidding should be a little more conservative, because the penalties for under-tricks are doubled. However, the object in bidding at all times should be to make game if it is at all possible. Here, of course, points already scored below the line must be taken into account. If you have already got 40 points, there is no need to bid above two hearts or spades or three clubs or diamonds, unless there is a chance of making a slam. You may, however, be forced to go higher if you are overbid by your opponents.

This leads on to what is called "defensive bidding". The object here is not so much to gain a good contract as to prevent the opponents from getting one. It is used especially against a part score, and to prevent the loss of a game or rubber a side may be justified in bidding slightly higher than their hands warrant. It is worth while to lose 100 points and save the game or rubber. Another possible result of defensive bidding is to make the other side bid above their strength, and thus just fail to make their contract. However, defensive bidding calls for care, especially when the side is vulnerable. To save the rubber at the expense of going down by three tricks when doubled and vulnerable—a cost of 800 points—is not worth while.

A word must be said about bidding for slam. This may seem very ambitious to beginners, and it is certainly galling to bid six and make only five (i.e. eleven tricks) when a call of four would have won game and possibly rubber. However, the fact is that no player can afford to ignore slam bidding, and it must be learnt. Slam hands are dealt every now and then, to both sides; and if only one side takes advantage of them, the other side must expect to forfeit a lot of points.

Another thing to remember is the use of the double. It is a powerful weapon, and the rewards for good doubling are high; but you should never double unless you are really confident of being able to defeat your opponents' contract. Be especially cautious if there is a freak distribution of the cards—you can tell this from your own hand—for this may mean that your aces will be trumped; and be wary if your partner has not taken any part in the bidding. If he has bid, you can count on a certain value in his hand, and this may enable you to make a shrewd double when it could not possibly be justified by your own hand alone; but if your partner has remained silent, do not double in the hope that he will be able to make "just a trick or so". He probably won't.

There is another thing about doubling. If you think that your opponents are likely to lose their contract only because they are in the wrong trump suit, but would probably make it in another suit, keep quiet. A double enables them to bid again, and afterwards they may thank you for the warning.

It need hardly be stated that there is great danger in "doubling into game"—that is, in doubling a contract such as two spades when your opponents have no part score. You should never make a double such as this unless you are really *sure* of making six tricks—and if you are as sure as that you can probably do better by overbidding.

Finally do not bid above the strength of your hand because of the temptation of the score card. You may

reach three spades in the bidding, and know that you have
little hope of making four; it is not clever to bid four
simply because you hate the idea of scoring 90 below
the line when you need only 100 for game. If you are
tempted to go too high in a bid to make game, count the
cost first—and remember that you may well be doubled.

The above general remarks on bidding are based on
common-sense principles, and hold good whatever particular system is adopted. To these may be added one
golden rule which should never be forgotten: Contract
Bridge is a partnership game. Do not bid on the strength
of your own hand alone. Consider it in relation to the
combined strength of your partner's hand and your own.
Similarly, do not assume your position is hopeless merely
because your own hand is weak; your partner may have
an excellent hand, and require only very little support
from you to bid for game.

How do you discover what your partner holds? How
do you tell him your own strength? The answer to this is
simply by your bidding.

Apart from exceptional cases, your first bid is not
normally intended to be your side's final contract. It is
intended to give your partner an idea of your strength
and to tell him your best suit. His reply will give you
similar information, and as the bidding goes on you will
gain a clearer picture of each other's hands. For this
reason you should keep the bidding at a low level, so
that you will have as many opportunities as possible for
exchanging information before you decide on your final
contract. You should only bid at a higher level than you
need if you want to show extra strength that was not
revealed in your first bid.

The choice of the trump suit is a matter for the
partnership, and you should realise that your own favourite may not fit with your partner's hand. You may have
four very good spades, but if your partner has only one
it is hardly likely to be your best suit. You have every
right to insist if you have a long, strong trump suit, but
otherwise you should try to find a suit that gets some
support from your partner.

As a basis for the exchange of information by bidding
you will have to adopt one of the many "systems" that
have been invented. Some of these are highly complex

codes, with artificial conventions. In one system, for example, an opening bid of "one club" or "two clubs" has no reference whatever to the club suit, but simply gives information on the general strength of the hand. In other systems the same bids have quite a different significance. It is therefore necessary that you should learn the main points of at least one of the popular systems, and keep to it. What is more important is that you and your partner should play to the same system, otherwise you will simply mislead each other.

There is not room here for a description of even the most popular systems, and the reader who intends to take up Contract seriously is advised to get one of the many books published on the subject. However, certain elements are common to all systems, and these will be discussed here.

In the first place, when you pick up your hand you make a valuation of it. This valuation is based on defensive strength—that is to say, on the number of tricks you are likely to make against your opponents' declaration. When you are defending you will probably take tricks only with Honour cards; when you are attacking, with your own choice of trump suit, you may expect to make tricks with low trumps and in long side suits. At the beginning of the bidding you have no idea whether you will eventually be attacking or defending.

There are two common ways of making this valuation. One is counting your "honour tricks", or "quick tricks". The other is by adding up points for the various Honour cards, according to a fixed scale. The two methods are different in application, but their effect is similar; and only one need be described. The "Honour trick" method is chosen because it is probably still the more general. It was invented by Ely Culbertson, the famous American bridge expert. The values are as follows:

An Ace counts as one Honour trick; Ace and King of the same suit count as two Honour tricks. King and Queen together count as one Honour trick; so do King, Jack and ten. Ace and Queen together count as one and a half Honour tricks, while half an Honour trick is allowed for any of the following: King and at least one other card of the same suit; Queen, Jack and one other card; King and Jack alone; Queen and another *and* Queen and another in two different suits. Certain other combinations receive "plus" values. Two plus values are equivalent to half an Honour trick, so a plus value may be considered as quarter of an Honour trick. In a combination of Ace, King and Queen of the same suit, the Queen is given a plus value; so is the Jack in a combination of King, Queen and Jack, or in Ace, Jack and another, or in King, Jack and another. Any singleton or void receives a plus value, but only one singleton or void may be counted in one hand.

Here are two examples of the way the Honour trick count works out:

(1) The hand is as follows: Spades: Ace, King, 3, 2; Hearts: 2; Diamonds: Ace, Queen, 5, 4; Clubs: King, Jack, 10, 6.

Honour trick count: Spades: 2; Hearts, plus; Diamonds: $1\frac{1}{2}$; Clubs: 1.—Total, $4\frac{1}{2}$ plus.

(2) The hand is as follows: Spades: Ace, King, Queen, Jack, 10, 9; Hearts: Jack, 5, 3; Diamonds: Queen, 7, 2; Clubs: King.

Honour trick count: Spades: 2 plus; Hearts: nil; Diamonds: nil; Clubs: plus.—Total, $2\frac{1}{2}$.

A comparison of these two counts shows why the Honour-trick valuation is defensive. If the Spades are trumps, the second hand holds six certain tricks, but if the opponents are declarers in another suit it is doubtful if even two tricks will be made in spades.

Under the Culbertson system, a player is required to hold at least two and a half Honour tricks before he can open the bidding. He need hold only one and a half to intervene in the bidding after it has been opened by an opponent; and little more than one honour trick to give mild support to a bid by his partner. A player holding five or more honour tricks will open with a strong bid of two of a suit—called the "forcing two", because the partner is required to bid in answer even if he holds no Honour tricks at all. In the latter case he would show his weakness by bidding two no-trumps. An opening bid of three indicates a long, strong trump suit containing at least six cards, but with little Honour trick strength in the hand. This bid is weaker than the forcing two, and may be passed by the player's partner.

These details are mentioned merely as examples, be-

cause in other systems the various bids have quite different meanings. An example of the wide divergences may
be seen in the opening one no-trump bid. In some systems
this indicates a good hand with at least three and a half
Honour tricks. In other systems it indicates a much
weaker hand. In yet other systems, one no-trump denotes
strength only when the side is vulnerable.

Bidding for slam is the subject of numerous special
conventions. The usual "invitation" to slam, made after
the customary exchange of information at low levels, is a
bid of four no-trumps. The reply depends upon the convention used. In the Blackwood Convention it is auto-
matic and simply announces the player's holding of Aces;
if he has no Aces he bids five Clubs; one Ace, five Diamonds; two Aces, five Hearts; three Aces, five Spades;
and four Aces, five no-trumps. This bid is entirely unre-
lated to any of the suits named. In the Culbertson "four-
five no-trump" convention, the question is quite different
and a different answer is expected. It is therefore clearly
vital that partners should agree on their slam convention
before play begins.

The playing of the hand in Contract Bridge resembles
Whist in many respects, but there are two important
differences. In the first place, one hand (dummy) is exposed to the view of the three players taking part; and,
secondly, each of the three players may know something
about the hands of the others because of the bidding
that preceded the final contract.

To take an obvious example, the player on the declarer's left, who has to make the first lead, may have no
natural lead in his own hand, and has the added difficulty
that dummy will not be exposed until after his lead has
been made; but in the course of the bidding his partner
called a certain suit, so he leads his highest card in that
suit. Sometimes a player will intervene in the bidding
merely in order to tell his partner what to lead if, as he
expects, the other side become the contractors.

Similarly the declarer can draw inferences from the
bidding of his opponents. If he is forced to finesse he may
be able to "place" the missing Honour by his opponents'
bidding.

As soon as dummy's cards are laid on the table the

declarer should count his losing tricks. (If the hand is played in no-trumps he should count his winning tricks.) If he sees that he can make the contract without difficulty, he should do so without further ado. It is never worth while taking even the slightest risk for the sake of making overtricks, the points value of which is very small unless the contract is doubled.

If the declarer foresees difficulties, he should consider them at the start. If he wants nine tricks and can make eight at once, he should not just play these off in the hope that the ninth will appear at the end. His very first consideration should be how to make that ninth trick. He must plan his campaign before covering the first lead.

There are certain conventions in the playing of Contract, and these are easily learnt. One is that the King should be led from Ace and King; the King should also be led from King and Queen. One should avoid leading from a suit headed by a "tenace" (e.g. Ace and Queen). The usual lead in a no-trumps Contract is the fourth highest card in the player's longest and strongest suit. Certain of the old Whist maxims hold good in Contract Bridge, although they should not be slavishly followed. One should return a partner's lead unless there are good reasons for making a different lead. There is safety in leading through strength to weakness. The higher card should be played from a doubleton unless it is an Honour.

The declarer will obviously want to draw trumps as soon as possible, and the fact that he must lose one or even two tricks in this suit should not deter him. However, he should not draw trumps if he thinks he can use any of those in the hand with the smaller holding. For example, if there are three small trumps in dummy, and a short side-suit, he may be able to make an additional trick by ruffing. The point to remember is that ruffing is of use only when it involves trumps that would not otherwise be made. If you hold six trumps in your own hand you do not gain anything by leading another suit from dummy and trumping. You would have made that trump anyway.

There are, however, certain circumstances when this kind of play may be your best line of attack. Suppose that spades are trumps, and that you know you are going to find it difficult to make your Contract. Honour cards and trumps alone will not give you enough tricks. However, there is a long side suit in dummy—seven hearts headed by the ace. The other Honour cards are missing. You have only one heart in your own hand.

You assume that you will probably lose the second and third tricks in hearts if you do not trump, so you play in the following way. First you play the ace from dummy, and this removes your own singleton heart. Then you lead another Heart from dummy, and trump in your own hand. You get back into dummy and lead another heart, and again trump—playing a card high enough to prevent the last player from over-trumping if you think he is likely to have no more Hearts. If the Hearts out against you were split three-two, they will now all have been played, so that the remaining four cards in the suit in dummy can only be beaten by a trump. So you draw trumps from your own hand, and then get back into dummy and play off the remaining hearts.

There is one danger and one difficulty in this play. The danger is of over-trumping by an opponent, and this will be much greater if the outstanding Hearts are badly split (e.g. four-one). The difficulty is getting back into dummy the necessary number of times. This latter difficulty occurs in many circumstances, and it is most important that in planning your campaign you should count your entry cards and look after them.

In seeking to make odd tricks it is usually better to try to establish low cards in a long side suit than to play the cross-ruffing game. Remember that even a four-card suit can be considered long; if the outstanding nine cards are evenly shared, the fourth assumes the value of an Ace once trumps have been drawn.

Do not try to finesse until there is no other way of making your odd trick. It is the weakest play. Many players excuse themselves for going down by saying they would have made the Contract "if the King had been sitting on the other side"; but often a way can be found of making the Contract irrespective of where the missing King is placed.

In no-trumps, of course, establishing low cards in long suits is of vital importance—and it is equally important to try to prevent your opponents from removing your "stoppers" in their long suits. It often pays to lose a trick in no-trumps for this purpose.

The player on your left opens the game by leading Hearts. You guess that the card is the fourth highest of his longest and strongest suit, and from the value of the card and previous bidding you decide that this player probably has at least five Hearts, possibly six. You and dummy have six between you, so that your other opponent is unlikely to have more than two. You have one stopper in Hearts—the Ace, in your own hand. All the other Honour cards are held by your opponents.

In these circumstances, even if the third player puts down the King, you should not take the first trick. Keep your ace for the second trick. Then, if the partner on your right gets the lead later, he will be unable to lead Hearts, and this may save you three tricks. In these circumstances, of course, you will do everything you can to prevent the player on your left from getting the lead; and if you must finesse, you will do it by leading from your own hand to dummy, so that if the finesse fails it will not open the way for those dangerous Hearts.

The playing of Contract Bridge, like the bidding, has been developed into something like a science, and this increases the balance of skill over luck in this game. Much can be learnt from books on Contract; but in playing more than bidding, the best teacher is experience.

CANASTA

CANASTA is one of the oldest and newest card games in the world. For many years it was played in South America, unnoticed by other countries; then suddenly it caught on in the U.S.A., and the craze spread like wildfire. Within a matter of a few years Canasta rose from obscurity to become one of the most popular card games in the world.

In the early days of the craze there was a lot of confusion over the rules, and there is still not the same general agreement over these as there is for Contract Bridge. The rules followed here are those as played at Crockford's Club, London, at the time of writing. These differ slightly from the rules of the Regency Club, New

York City, and they may be modified in the future. However, it is unlikely that there will be any basic change now that a standard for the game has been provided.

Canasta is a game of the Rummy family, and it is quite easy to learn. It differs from Rummy in two important respects: one is that sequences do not count, so that no attention is paid to suits; the other is that although the procedure for "going out" is similar, this is not the main object of the game. Indeed, when winning, the object is to prolong the game as long as possible; and to end the deal by going out is a purely defensive measure.

There are other differences between Canasta and the various Rummy games—for example, there is no playing on opponents' exposed cards. The scoring, too, is entirely different. So while it may be said that Canasta resembles Rummy, the new player with experience of Rummy has no advantage over other beginners. It will therefore be treated here as an entirely separate game.

Canasta can be played as a partnership game by four, five, or six players; or it may be played without partners by two or three players.

The game is played with two packs of cards together with four jokers—108 cards altogether. Most packs of cards are sold with a joker and a blank card, and the latter can be used as the second joker. The two packs do not need to be of the same colour. Before the first deal they are shuffled together.

The four jokers and the eight twos are all called "wild cards," and they may be used as cards of any other denomination. The eight threes are special cards, which will be explained later. All the others are "natural cards".

The object of the game is to make "melds" and especially "canastas". A meld is made when three or more cards of the same rank—for example, three nines or three Queens—are placed face up on the table. A meld must contain at least two natural cards, and not more than three wild cards.

A canasta is a meld of seven or more cards of the same rank. It must contain at least four natural cards.

There is one exception to the rule about the number of wild cards allowed in a meld. Wild cards may be added to any completed canasta, even if it already contains three wild cards.

A completed canasta is placed on the table in a stack. The top card must be face upwards, and it should be red if the canasta is "natural" (that is, contains only natural cards), and black if it is a "mixed" canasta (that is, if it contains wild as well as natural cards). If a wild card is added to a completed natural canasta, it becomes mixed and the red card at the top should be replaced by a black one.

Before the play is described it is necessary to say something about the scoring. In the first place, each card has a fixed value. A Joker counts 50 points; an Ace or two, 20 points; every card from King down to eight, 10 points; and every card from seven down to black three, 5 points. The red threes have a special value which will be explained later.

So a mixed canasta of eights, containing four natural cards and three wild cards, of which one is a Joker, and two are twos, is worth the following: 4 x 10 plus 50 plus 2 x 20 = 40 plus 50 plus 40 = 130.

Cards count in favour of a player only when they are exposed on the table in canastas and melds. All the cards that are still held in his hand at the end of play count against him, their total points value being subtracted from his score. A meld or canasta is made only when the cards are placed face upward on the table, and they cannot be put down after play ends. You are not obliged to meld at any time, and there are good reasons for refraining from doing so in the course of the play: but if you are left at the end with, say, three eights *in your hand,* the 30 points count against you.

In addition to these points, there are valuable bonuses, and these dictate the nature of the play. The bonus for going out is 100; for going out concealed—that is, placing all the cards from a hand on the table at one time, in a number of melds and at least one canasta—the bonus is 200; for every mixed canasta the bonus is 300; and for every natural canasta, 500. This explains clearly why the object of the game is to get as many canastas as possible rather than to go out before the opponents.

Game is 5,000 points, and there is an extra bonus of 500 for making the game.

In describing the play the four-handed game will be described first, as this is the most popular. First there is the cut for partners and then the deal, made in the way described on page 9. Players cutting identical cards or the Joker must cut again. Only eleven cards are dealt to each player. The remainder of the pack, called the "stock", is put in the middle of the table, and the top card is placed face upward beside it. This is the first card of the "discard pile".

If this card happens to be a wild card or a red three, the next card is turned over to cover it. If more than one red three *and* one wild card are turned up, any further such cards are not placed on the discard pile, but are buried in the stock. Play cannot begin until the top card of the discard pile is a natural card.

If the face card is a black three it is similarly covered before play begins.

Now the first player draws a card, which he adds to his hand; then, if he is able and willing, he melds; finally, he discards on the top of the discard pile. The next player repeats the process, and so it goes on throughout the game. Drawing is compulsory; melding is optional; discarding is compulsory except when a player goes out, when he may discard, but need not do so. Each new discard must completely conceal all the other cards in the discard pile.

If a player will have only one card left in his hand after discarding, he must announce "one card" before making the discard. He may ask any other player how many cards he holds, and he may count the cards left in the stock.

The player must draw either the top card of the stock or the top card of the discard pile. If he takes the latter, he must also take all the cards underneath it—the whole of the pile. This is compulsory.

The discard pile may be taken only if the top card is used in a meld, and the meld must be made at once. The correct procedure is as follows:—

The player puts the other cards for the meld face upwards on the table, together with any other melds that he is making at the same time. Then he picks up the discard pile and adds the top card to the rest of the meld on the table. The rest of the pile becomes part of his hand. He makes his discard, which becomes the start of a new discard pile, and play continues.

For the first meld by a partnership the discard pile

C

may be taken only if the player has in his hand at least two natural cards of the same rank as the top card of the discard pile.

There is a further condition regarding the first meld for each partnership. It can be made only when the meld or melds to be made add up to a minimum points score, and this depends on the partnership's score in the game so far. If they have a minus score, there is no minimum for the first meld; if they have less than 1,500 points, the minimum required is 50; if they have 1,500 or over, but less than 3,000, the minimum is 90; if they have 3,000 or over, the minimum is 120. This is a form of handicap to help the players who are behind in the score.

So if you have scored 1,000 points, and the top card of the discard pile is, say, a ten, you may not use it to make the first meld with only two tens from your own hand, as the points count of this meld would be only 30. If, however, you also hold in your hand, say, two fours and a two (points value 30), and are willing to make this meld at the same time, then you may take the discard pile.

If, however, you wish to use the top card of the discard pile to complete a canasta as your first meld, no minimum points count is required.

A player is not obliged to take the discard pile to make his first meld. He may instead draw a card from the stock and then meld out of his own hand—but, of course, the minimum points count must still be observed unless the first meld is a complete canasta. Here, as always, cards must be melded before the discard is made.

Subsequent melds by either partner may be made either from the hand or with the top card of the discard pile; if the latter is taken, of course, the whole of the pile must be taken into the hand. There is no minimum points count after the first meld, nor is it necessary to have two natural cards to match the top card of the discard pile; one natural card and a wild card will suffice (unless the pack is frozen—this will be explained later).

In addition, after the first meld the discard pile may be taken by either partner if the top card is added to a meld already made by the side. The only exception is that the top card may not be used to add to a completed canasta. (Again, this privilege is lost if the pack is frozen.)

A player holding only one card may not take a discard pile consisting of only one card.

The pack is said to be frozen when any player discards a wild card. The discard pile may then be taken only by a player who can put down two *natural* cards to meld with the top card of the pile. In other words, the rules for obtaining the discard pack are the same as they were for the first meld of a partnership, except that no minimum points count is required.

The pack is said to be self-frozen if, immediately after the deal, the card turned up is either a wild card or a red three, which has to be covered in the manner already explained. A self-frozen pack is regarded in the same way as a frozen pack; so that if, for example, a player makes his first meld out of his own hand, he still needs two natural cards to match the top card of the discard pile before he can take it.

The first wild card or red three that freezes the pack is placed half under, and at right angles to, the discard pile.

When a player freezes the pack the next player may not take the discard pile in any circumstances; that is, he may not take it by melding with the wild card or with the card that is left at the top of the discard pile (which must have been discarded by the player on the right of the player who froze the pack).

At any time during the play a player may, after drawing a card and before discarding, add natural and wild cards to the melds already made by the partnership. In this way melds can be built up into canastas. When a player takes the discard pile he may use any cards in it to add to his side's melds (including the meld that he has just made with the top card of the discard pile) immediately before discarding. But he cannot *change* cards in melds or canastas; for example, he cannot substitute a natural for a wild card. Once a wild card has been included in a meld it cannot be taken out of it.

A few words may now be said about red threes. These are bonus cards, although they may also be penalty cards.

After each deal, the first thing each player does when it is his turn to play is to put down on the table, face upwards, any red threes he may hold, and draw an equivalent number of cards from the stock. Subsequently, when a player draws a red three from the stock, he follows exactly the same procedure.

When a player takes a discard pile that was self-frozen by a red three, he places that red three on the table, but does not draw a replacement from the stock.

If a player fails to draw a replacement for a red three when it is his turn to play, he loses the right to that replacement. If he fails to place a red three on the table at the first opportunity, he may correct his mistake when it is his next turn, without penalty. But if the hand ends before the correction is made, he loses 500 points for each red three in his hand.

When play ends, each partnership that has melded is awarded 100 points for each red three that either partner has placed on the table; if all four red threes are held by one side, the bonus for these is 800 points. However, if a partnership has not made even one meld—which means that all the points values in their hands will count against them—then the bonus for red threes (100 for each, 800 for four) is also *deducted* from their score.

Black threes also are special cards, but no bonus attaches to them. A black three is a "stop" card. When it is discarded it may not be picked up by the next player in any circumstances—not even if he holds two black threes in his own hand. But a black three does not freeze the pack. Its effect lasts for only one turn in the game—that is, until it is covered by the next discard.

When a black three turns up as the face card immediately after the deal, it is covered by another card from the stock, but the pack is not self-frozen.

Black threes may be melded only by a player when he is going out. Even then they may not be melded with a wild card.

A player is said to go out when he melds every card in his hand, with the exception of one that he may want to discard, although he is not obliged to do so. A player may not go out until his side has made at least one canasta or unless he is making a canasta in going out.

Before melding or indicating a possible meld, a player may ask the question, "Partner, may I go out?" If he asks the question before drawing, he may draw from either the stock or the discard pile. He is not bound to ask the question before going out, but if he does so his partner must reply either "Yes" or "No", and his answer must be carried out.

If a player melds any card and then asks the question, he must go out whatever the answer. If, after asking the question but before getting a reply, the player melds or gives any information—or if his partner says "No", but gives any information—then either opponent may demand that the player either does or does not go out.

If, as a result of asking the question, a player is obliged to go out but states that he cannot, he has to place all his cards on the table, melding where he can; and all the cards that are unmelded are considered as penalty cards.

Penalty cards remain on the table, face upwards, until play ends. The player can treat them as part of his hand for the purpose of melding or taking the discard pile, and they may thus be used by themselves or with cards remaining in the player's hand. When the hand ends, unmelded penalty cards are counted as in the player's hand.

At each turn to play, the player must discard one of his penalty cards, until such time as all of them have been either melded or discarded.

When a player draws the last card of the stock and discards without going out, the next player may take the discard. If he does not, play ends. If he takes the discard, play ends with his discard. If he does not go out, then the hand ends, the scores are counted, and there is no going out bonus.

There are certain penalties for irregularities. If a player takes the top card of a discard pile and finds he cannot meld it, he is penalised 50 points and the card is replaced. If, in drawing from the stock, he sees or exposes any cards, he must show them to all the players and replace them. The next player may shuffle the pack if he wishes.

If a player mixes the discard pile with his hand before melding the top card, his entire hand must be placed face upward on the table. The discard pile is reconstructed as far as possible—with the opponents making the decision on doubtful points—and the player's original cards become penalty cards.

A meld is said to be illegal if a player puts down cards

for a first meld with an insufficient points count; if he puts down cards that are inadequate to take the discard pile (e.g. one matching card and a wild card when the pack is frozen); if he puts down all his cards for going out after having got the answer "No" to his question, "Partner, may I go out?"; or if he tries to go out when his partnership has not got one complete canasta and he cannot make one.

If attention is drawn to an illegal meld such as one of the above before the player concerned has discarded, he may correct his mistake—if he can—by rearranging the melds or adding more cards. Any cards that are not made into a legal meld become penalty cards.

If the next player completes his play before attention is drawn to an illegal meld, there is no penalty, and the illegal meld is regarded as if it had been legal; so a first meld with an insufficient points count would be held a correct meld.

If a player draws from the stock out of turn, at his next turn he must discard without drawing, and he is penalised 100 points. If he tries to take the discard pile out of turn, any cards he has put down become penalty cards, and he is also penalised 100 points.

At the end of a hand each side adds up its score. It is reckoned in two parts: firstly, the basic score of bonuses (for canastas, red threes, and going out), less any penalties; secondly, the point score, being the points value of all melded cards less the points for cards left in the hands.

Here is the Canasta scoring table:

BONUSES

Natural canasta . . .	500
Mixed canasta . . .	300
Red three . . .	100
Four red threes on one side .	800
Going out	100
Going out concealed .	200
For the game (5,000 points) .	500

NOTE: The 200 bonus for going out concealed is instead of, not in addition to, the 100 for going out.

POINT VALUES

Joker	.	.	.	.	.	50
Ace	.	.	.	.	.	20
Two	.	.	.	.	.	20
King, Queen, Jack, 10, 9 or 8					.	10
7, 6, 5, 4, or black 3		.		.	.	5

So much for the rules and scoring in Canasta. As regards playing tactics, much contradictory advice has been given, but there are certain general principles that can be safely followed.

In the first place, you must decide at the beginning whether to play for the pack, and try to prolong the game and make as many canastas as you can, or whether to try to go out quickly. Playing for the pack offers chances of a bigger score, but you need the right sort of hand for it. You want at least one set of three or more of a kind, and two or perhaps three (not more) wild cards.

If, on the other hand, you start with four or more wild cards, you will probably do better to try to go out quickly and catch your opponents before they have made a canasta.

In either case you must be prepared to change your tactics according to the run of the play.

If you are playing for the pack, do not be in too much of a hurry to make the first meld. It has advantages, of course—it gives your partner a chance to lay off cards on your melds, and it opens the pack to you. But the pack will probably be closed again, for your opponents will usually freeze the pack at once, unless they too can make their first meld.

When the pack is frozen it is harder to take, and it soon begins to grow to a considerable size. The players with the larger hands always have the better chance of taking it in the end—and so, when you meld, do so economically, putting down as few cards as you possibly can.

For this reason you should be careful not to take the pack if it is going to mean reducing the number of cards in your own hand as a result of melding.

Once you succeed in capturing a big pack you have everything in your favour for capturing another. All you need do is to meld sparingly, and always keep more cards in your hand than are held by your left-hand opponent. Do not think of going out, and do not complete canastas with wild cards unless there is a danger of your opponents going out. The longer the hand goes on, the more canastas you are likely to make.

Watch your discards. Watch what your left-hand opponent discards, and try to find out the cards that are safe to put down. A black three is a useful card to hold for a round or two, and then use when you are most anxious to gain time and make sure your opponent will not get the pack.

As the pack grows, you must seek ever safer discards. You may have to break up a set of three or more in your hand to provide discards.

There may be another reason for breaking up a set of three, and this is called "advertising". You throw off one of your set, in the hope that the opponent on your right will think that a card of the same rank will be a "safe" discard for him to throw.

If you are playing to go out quickly, never mind about the pack. Do not fight for it, and do not worry about discarding cards that may help your opponents. Get your melds down, but use as few wild cards as possible.

When your opponents gain control of the pack your best policy is to run for cover, to try to go out quickly. At least you may be able to cut your losses. Don't compete for the pack; put down your melds to help your partner complete the canasta that is needed before either of you can go out. Going out in this case is a purely defensive measure, aimed at ending the hand before your opponents can build up many canastas.

Freezing the pack is another defensive move. It is usually done to check the opponents from acquiring more and more cards by taking the discard pile. When you freeze the pack you can now safely discard cards of the same rank as your opponents' existing melds and canastas, for it is unlikely that either will also hold a pair in his hand. So you have bought time—at the expense of a wild card—and you and your partner will probably use it in an effort to go out before the frozen pack is captured by your opponents.

Memory plays a big part in Canasta. When each new discard goes down, the rest of the pile is concealed. It pays to know what is in that pile—and it pays to watch the discards of both your opponents and your partner.

Two-handed Canasta is played under exactly the same rules as those that have been described for the four-handed game, except that all references to partnership should be ignored, and that more cards are dealt at the beginning of the hand. The most popular variation is for each player to be dealt fifteen cards, and in this game two canastas are needed before a player can go out. Alternatively, each player may be dealt thirteen cards, in which case only one canasta is needed.

Yet a further alternative is for each player to be dealt fifteen cards and then to draw an extra card at every turn to play. Thus when a player draws from the stock, he takes two cards instead of one; when he takes the discard pile, he must also take one card from the stock. Only one card is discarded at each turn. Two canastas are needed before going out.

Quite different tactics are needed for playing the two-handed game. Your first object must be to get more cards in your hand than your opponent holds, and the only way you can do this is by taking the discard pile. The golden rule, therefore, is not to make your initial meld unless by so doing you increase the number of cards in your hand. This means that you should never make the first meld from your own hand, and should take the discard pile only if it is large enough to leave you with more cards than you are going to use for the meld. You have no partner to think about, so do not meld anything from your own hand except canastas.

After the first meld, do not meld anything unless it is to take the pack—and only then if the pack contains more cards than you started with, after you have made the necessary meld.

The more cards you acquire, the easier it will be to find safe discards. Black threes are very valuable cards in the two-handed game, but they should be saved for discarding when the pile has become big. When the pile is small, make dangerous discards, for it will suit you if your opponent takes a small pack.

Most of the cards in the discard pile can be regarded as safe discards: either you threw them down and your opponent did not want them, or he discarded them himself. But beware of "advertising" on his part. A safer discard is from a long set in your own hand. If, for example, you have six Jacks, and you have gained more cards than your opponent and are therefore on the offensive, use these as discards. The chances are that you will get them back by taking the pile yourself.

If you are on the defensive—that is, if your opponent has gained more cards than you—you should try to get out as soon as possible. This is not easy, because freezing the pack is of less use in the two-handed game, and it is especially difficult if you have to make two canastas before going out. The defensive player should concentrate on trying to make these canastas, and should not worry about discarding cards that his opponent is likely to take.

Three-handed Canasta is, like two-handed Canasta, a non-partnership game. It may be played with either thirteen or eleven cards. Tactics are similar to those used for the two-handed game, except in discarding. Here you must watch the discards of the player on your left, in the same way as in the four-handed game.

Five-handed Canasta is a game between two sides, one of two players and the other of three. However, only four hands are dealt, as one of the team of three must sit out. Procedure is as follows:

The players cut for partners in the usual way. Let us call the player who cut the highest card A, the one who cut the next highest B, and so on down to E. Now the game will be played between A, B, and C on the one hand, and D and E on the other. D and E will play as partners in every hand.

For the first hand A and B will play, and C will sit out. For the second hand C will come in and B will sit out; and for the third hand B will come back and play with C while A sits out. This rotation continues till the end of the game. The player sitting out is not allowed to give advice to his partners or to make any comment during the play of the hand, but he may point out any error in the score at the end.

Six-handed Canasta is similar to five-handed Canasta, except that here the game is between two teams of three players each. This means that one player from each team will have to sit out for each hand, and the rotation is as in the five-handed game.

Alternatively, all six players can take active part at the same time, in which case the game will be played between three teams each of two partners. If the partners are A and B, C and D, E and F respectively, they will be seated at the table in the order A-C-E-B-D-F.

CRIBBAGE

CRIBBAGE is an old-fashioned but quite good game, of which there are several variations.

Usually, it is regarded as a game for two players; but three or four may play, if desired. The varieties are "five-card", "six-card" and "seven-card" cribbage, of which the first-named is the most commonly played.

The rules and methods of play are quite different from those of games of the Whist family: there are no trumps

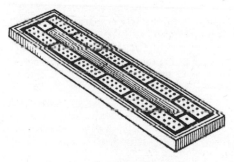

Fig. 8.—A Cribbage board

or tricks, and the whole business of the game consists of making various combinations of cards which score points either by reason of their similarity (e.g. pairs) or because their values added together make a certain figure.

The score is kept by means of a Cribbage board and

pegs (see Fig. 8). The board has two lines of holes on each side, with thirty holes in each. At each end of the board there is a central hole called "game hole". The lines of holes are divided into sets of five to facilitate counting. When points are scored the *hindmost* peg is moved forward the requisite number of holes beyond the front peg. Both players start from the same end of the board, and the first to reach "game hole" wins, whatever may be the stage of the game (i.e. the last hand need not necessarily be played out).

An ordinary pack of fifty-two cards is used. The Ace is the lowest card. Other cards rank in the usual order, but in "counting" the court cards (King, Queen, Jack) are counted as "tens".

Briefly, the method of play is for each player to throw out a card (or two in some variations) from his hand into what is called the "Crib". Then the hands are played, points being scored during play. After the play each player's hand is displayed and further points scored. And finally the "crib" (taken by each player in turn) is displayed and further points scored by one or other of the players.

For the purpose of illustration, let us take the "five-card" variation as played by two players. The players cut for deal, the lowest being dealer. Five cards are dealt, one at a time, to each player. The dealer in each hand is the player to have the "crib" of that hand.

As a compensation for non-crib, the non-dealer scores three points. The remainder of the cards, undealt, are placed face down between the players. Each player now discards two of his cards to form the "crib". This having been done, the non-dealer cuts the pack by lifting a portion of the cards. The card immediately beneath the cut is then faced up on the pack. This is known as the "turn-up". If it is a Jack, the dealer scores "two" for "his heels".

In the play of the hands points may be scored for pairs, pair-royals, and double pair-royals; for runs of three, four, five; seven, eight, nine, etc.; and for making "fifteen" or "thirty-one". (Pairs are cards of equal rank, e.g. two Jacks. "Pair-royals", or "triplets", are three cards of equal rank, e.g. three sixes. "Double pair-royals" are four cards of equal rank, e.g. four Queens.) For pairs, two points are scored; for pair-royals, six; for double pair-royals, twelve; for runs of three or four, three or four points, as the case may be; and for making "fifteen" or "thirty-one", two points. A single point may be made for "a go", that is, a player plays a card, which with the others previously played makes the count so near to thirty-one that the other player is unable to play a further card that will not make it greater than thirty-one; the first player then scores a "go", one point. In five-card Crib the cards are not played beyond the point of thirty-one in total count for any one hand.

Let us illustrate. A is the dealer. It is therefore B's turn to play. He plays a "four". Now it is evident that A cannot play any card, whose value added to the four will make fifteen; the most he can play is ten. We will suppose B's hand contains a four, a seven, and a nine, whilst A's contains a four, a six, and a "tenth card" (King, Queen, Jack, or ten). A four having been played by B, it is for A to consider his best play. He cannot make fifteen, but he can score "a pair" by playing a four and saying, "eight for a pair". He does so, and pegs two points. B replies with his seven, making in all fifteen. He says "fifteen for two", and pegs his two points. A now replies with his "ten" card, saying "twenty-five". A cannot play, since his nine would make over thirty-one, therefore he says "go". A, however, has a card which exactly makes "thirty-one", for which he scores two points. If his card had been a "three" making twenty-eight, he would have scored one only for the "go".

Similarly, if in the play of a hand A starts with a four, B replies with a five (very bad play ordinarily), and A then puts on a six, the total is fifteen for two, and a run of three, five (three extra points for the run). But if now B has a seven, he calls "twenty-two for four", the run of four (four, five, six, seven) scoring four points. It will be seen at once, therefore, that to play cards which may enable the opponent to make pairs, or fifteens, or the beginnings of runs, is bad, unless other cards are held which will enable the first player to score the pair-royal, six points, or double pair-royal, twelve points, or a run of three or four, as the case may be.

Having played the hand, the "show" begins. The non-dealer has the first show. The cards are turned up and points reckoned for fifteens, pairs, pair-royals, or runs in the hand, counting in with it the turn-up. Two points are reckoned for each fifteen, and the cards may be counted for fifteen as many times as fresh combinations can be made. Let us assume another hand, in which three fives are held with a Jack turned up. Now it is evident that the three fives themselves make a fifteen. But in addition to this each of them will, in combination with the Jack turn-up, make another fifteen. The score goes then thus: fifteen-two (for three fives), fifteen-four for the first five and the Jack, fifteen-six for the second five and Jack, fifteen-eight for the third five and the Jack. For the pair-royal six, or fourteen points in all for that hand. The other hand contains a four, five, and six. These three cards make a fifteen, that is, fifteen-two; the five and the Jack score fifteen-four, and the sequence or run another three points, seven in all. Now we will assume, for demonstration, that with the same hands the turn-up was a five; there could not of course be such a turn-up, as there are only four fives, and the second hand would be different, but we will let that pass. The scores would then have been, for the first hand, fifteen-eight, and twelve for the double pair-royal, twenty in all. The four fives, Diamonds, Hearts, Clubs and Spades, may be counted four times in this way for the fifteen-eight; Diamond, Heart, Club; Diamond, Heart, Spade; Heart, Club, Spade; Diamond, Club, Spade. The other hand would be twelve. Fifteen-two, fifteen-four, two runs of three (six), making ten, and a pair, twelve.

When the cards of the hand, whether a run or not, are all of the same suit, the "flush" is counted in addition three points. In the crib a flush is only counted when the turn-up is also of the same suit. It is then five. Counting for crib, which always belongs to the dealer, follows the lines of that indicated for the hand, but as there are five cards in all to be reckoned, the points may be much higher than the hands. In discarding for crib there are two principles to be observed. Make up with the best cards you can spare from your hand, if it is your own crib; if it is your opponent's crib, throw out cards that will block him. It is evident that two cards of close value—a four and a five, or a seven and an eight—are good cards to throw into your own crib. The last two make a fifteen and only want one other, above or below, to make a run of three also. The five is a good card to throw out, since there is very much more chance of a "ten" card turning up than any other. To block your opponent, a nine and a King are good examples. Anything that will turn up as good for one will do no good to the other. It is impossible almost to contemplate two cards of the run being thrown out by your opponent and the necessary intervening card being turned up as well to complete it.

If the hand or crib contains the Jack of the turn-up suit, "one for his nob" is scored by the holder.

In the three-handed game, if played as five-card Cribbage, four cards are dealt to each player, one of which only is to be discarded. The fourth card, to complete the crib, is dealt last beside the pack.

In the six-card game, whether played as a single or by partners, after "thirty-one" or "go" is scored, the cards which have been played are turned over, and the game proceed as before. The first card to be played, if a seven, is seven; an eight played to it scores fifteen-two, and so on. The player who plays the last card scores one for it—"one for the last". With six-card crib the greatest number of cards to be held, either in hand or crib, will be five, and the best score for this will be twenty-nine, made by three fives and a Jack in hand or crib, the Jack to be of the same suit as the five of the turn-up. The counting then is, for the four fives together in various combinations, as detailed before, fifteen-eight, each of them again in combination with the Jack, another fifteen-eight, sixteen in all, twelve for the double pair-royal, twenty-eight, and "one for his nob".

If the six-card game is played as "three-handed", each player discards *one* to the crib, the full number of the crib (four) being made up by a card dealt from the pack. Thus each player has five cards in his hand, which, with the turn-up making six, renders very high scores possible. When, however, the six-card game is played single-handed there are only four cards to the hand, because each player puts two to the crib. In the four-handed (partner) game each player puts one—and remains with five cards in hand, as at the three-handed game.

Seven-card Cribbage is played single-handed. It is never played three-handed or four-handed. Two cards, to make up a crib of four cards, are put into the crib by each player. The hands are then as at the three-handed six-card game; i.e. five cards, with the turn-up making six.

The customary "game" scores for the different variations are:—

Five-card: 61 points (once up and down the board).

Six-card: 121 points (twice up and down the board).

Three- and four-handed six-card and seven-card: 181 points (three times up and down the board).

In assessing the values of the cards to be kept in the hand, regard must be given to three points: small cards are better for the play of the hand in making "fifteens", "goes", or "thirty-ones"; a "tenth" card is the most likely to turn up; odd cards are more likely to score for "show" than even ones. No hard and fast rules, therefore, can be laid down. Each card must be considered not only individually but in combination with its fellows, and in its relation to the prospective turn-up.

Cribbage is a game that affords ample material for thought, and exercise for quick calculation. Practice is the secret of success in this as in nearly all card games. To assist the learner, some of the leading hands for scoring points are given as examples:—

With four cards: *Points*

Four fives	Fifteen eight and a double pair-royal . 20
Three fives and a ten . .	Fifteen eight and a pair-royal . . 14
Two fives, a four, and a six . Two fours, a five, and a six . Two sixes, a four, and a five .	Fifteen four, pair, and double run of three . 12
Three threes and a nine . Three sixes and a nine . Three sixes and a three . Three sevens and an eight . Three eights and a seven . Three nines and a six . . Three sevens and an Ace .	Fifteen six and a pair-royal . . 12
Two eights, a six (or nine) and a seven . . . . Two sevens, a six, and an eight . . . . Six, five, and two fours .	Fifteen four, pair, and double run of three . 12

With four cards: *Points*

Two fives and two tens, or two court cards of like denomination . . .	Fifteen eight and two pairs . . .	12
Two nines and two sixes .	Fifteen eight and two pairs . . .	12
Two fives, a ten, and a court card . . .	Fifteen eight and a pair	10
Two sixes, a seven, and an eight	Fifteen two, pair, and double run of three .	10
A five and three court cards, or a ten and two court cards in sequence . . .	Fifteen six and run of three . . .	9
Any sequence of three cards, with a duplicate of one of them, but no "fifteen" .	Pair and double run of three .	8

With five cards:

Four threes and a nine . .	Fifteen twelve and a double pair-royal .	24
Three fives, a four, and a six	Fifteen eight, a pair-royal, and run of three thrice repeated . .	23
Three fours, a five, and a six; three sixes, a four, and a five; three sevens, an eight, and a nine; three eights, a seven, and a nine . .	Fifteen six, a pair-royal, and run of three thrice repeated . .	21
Two sixes, two sevens, and an eight; two sevens, an eight, and two nines; two eights, a seven, and two nines .	Fifteen four, two pairs, and run of three four times repeated . .	20
Three tens, or court cards, and two fives; three threes and two nines; three sevens and two Aces . . .	Fifteen twelve, pair-royal, and pair . .	20
Three threes and two sixes .	Fifteen ten, pair, and pair-royal . . .	18

The last score given on the previous page is made up as follows. First regard the three threes as nine. This, in combination with each of the two sixes, makes fifteen-four, the two sixes together make twelve, and each of the threes will now make a fifteen, six extra, fifteen-ten in all.

Three fours, three, and a five	Fifteen two, pair-royal, and run of three thrice repeated . . .	17
Any three cards in sequence, with duplicates of two of them, but no "fifteen" . }	Two pairs and run of three four times repeated . . .	16
Any three cards in sequence, with one of them thrice repeated, but no "fifteen" . }	Pair-royal, and run of three thrice repeated .	15

BEZIQUE

BEZIQUE is primarily a game for two players—and is one of the best of such games. As is usual, however, there are variations in which three or four players may play.

FIG. 9.—The order of the cards at Bezique

Two packs of thirty-two cards (known as Piquet packs) are used. In these there are no twos, threes, fours, fives or sixes. The cards rank as follows: Ace, *ten*, King, Queen, Jack, nine, eight, seven.

After the two packs are thoroughly shuffled together the players cut for deal. It is customary to give the highest card the preference, and also to rank the cards, in cutting, in the same way as in the game itself. Thus the player who cuts a ten will have the deal, unless his adversary cuts an Ace or another ten—whereupon they cut again.

Eight cards are dealt to each player (usually by threes, twos, and threes): the seventeenth card is turned up as trump and placed face upwards between the players. The remainder of the cards are placed face downwards beside the trump, and are known as the "stock".

The main object of each player is to score points by "declaring" the various combinations of cards set out in the list below, which also gives their scoring values.

Points

Common marriage (King and Queen of same suit) . 20
Royal marriage (King and Queen of trumps) . . 40
Single bezique (Queen of Spades and Jack of Diamonds) 40
Double bezique (same combination again declared in the course of same hand, by the same player, but with fresh cards) 500
Four Jacks duly declared 40
Four Queens duly declared 60
Four Kings duly declared 80
Four Aces duly declared 100
Sequence of five best trumps (Ace, King, Queen, Jack, ten) 250

In order to score these points the necessary cards must be all at the same time in the player's hand, and must be duly "declared" and laid upon the table. The exact process will become clearer when the play is explained.

In addition, however, to these scores a player may score points for the following, as indicated.

Points

For the seven of trumps, either turned up as trump by the dealer, or duly declared in the play . . . 10
For the second seven of trumps duly declared . . 10
For the "last" trick 10
For what are known as "brisques", viz. every Ace or ten appearing in the tricks in the course of play.

The winner of the trick scores 10 points for each brisque.

The seven of trumps, when declared, may be exchanged for the trump card.

A "game" is usually a thousand points. The score is

kept by means of bezique markers (see Fig. 10), which have two small dials with metal pointers—one dial showing points by tens up to a hundred, and the other by hundreds up to a thousand.

One of the peculiarities of Bezique is that although there is a trump suit, and a player may win tricks by "trumping", he is under *no obligation* (except for the last eight tricks) *to follow suit* if he can.

The non-dealer has first lead. If the dealer plays a higher card of the same suit, or a trump, he wins the trick, and may thereupon "declare" any of the above combina-

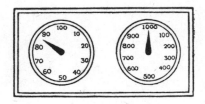

FIG. 10.—A Bezique marker

tions which he happens to hold, scoring the appropriate number of points. No points are scored for the actual winning of the tricks. No declaration can be made unless the declarer has just won a trick. The cards declared are laid face upwards on the table in front of him; but they still form part of his hand and may be led or played to tricks exactly as those still remaining in his hand.

If the cards laid down form two combinations, e.g. King and Queen of Spades and Jack of Diamonds, the player may only *score* one combination at that time, although he should *declare* both. The three cards mentioned form bezique and a marriage, and the player would say, "I score forty for bezique and twenty to score." The twenty points for marriage may be scored the next time the player wins a trick.

The winner of the first trick having made his declaration (if any) he takes the top card of the "stock" into his hand. His opponent takes the next, and the play proceeds as before.

It should be noted that a player holding an Ace or ten

cannot score anything for it (alone) while it is in his hand: to score a brisque it must be played to and win a trick.

Note also that a card which has been once used to make a given combination cannot be again used to form part of a similar combination: e.g. a Queen once "married" may not be married again, but she may form part of a sequence, or bezique. Further, no card that has been declared in any combination can again be declared in a combination of *lower value.*

When, by drawing cards after each trick, the stock eventually becomes exhausted, the method of play changes. Players now must follow suit if they can (penalty for revoke being 250 points), and the last eight tricks are for this reason known as "the Whist tricks". No more declarations can be made after the last card of stock has been drawn, and the only method of scoring is now by means of brisques, and winning of the last trick.

The following example will make the method of play clear: —

Suppose A is dealer and turns up the Queen of Hearts as trump.

B leads nine of Spades, and A takes it with the ten of the same suit, thereby scoring ten for a brisque. He also "declares", by laying on the table the Queen and King of Diamonds, a marriage, and scores twenty in respect of it. He then draws a card from the top of the stock, and adds it to those in his hand, and B follows his example.

A leads the eight of Diamonds, B takes it with the nine, and forthwith "declares" the seven of trumps, scoring ten in respect of it, and exchanging it for the Queen of Hearts turned up, which thenceforward becomes part of his hand. He draws another card from the stock and A does likewise.

B leads the eight of Spades. A plays to it the eight of Clubs, leaving the trick to B. B declares a royal marriage with the King and Queen of Hearts, for which he scores forty.

Fresh draw on either side. B leads the seven of Diamonds. A takes it with the Ace, securing another brisque, and declares bezique (Queen of Spades and Jack of Diamonds), scoring forty.

The game continues in like manner until the "stock", with the exception of one card and the seven of trumps, which was substituted for the turn-up, is exhausted. There is now a struggle to secure the next trick (last before the exhaustion of the stock), for it carries with it important advantages. It enables the winner to "declare" for the last time, and it gives him the lead for the last eight tricks. Having made his last declaration the winner of the trick draws the last card of the stock and his opponent takes the seven of trumps. The eight remaining tricks are played out, each player making what brisques he can, and saving a good card wherewith to capture the ten points carried by the last trick.

Bezique is by no means so simple as it looks, and there is a great deal more in the game than is at first apparent. Considerable discretion is required as to when a combination should be declared. If declared as soon as possible there is the disadvantage that your opponent is guided in his own play by seeing your cards. On the other hand, if delayed too long, your declarations may never be made, because your opponent may win, say, the last four or five of the "stock" tricks (i.e. the tricks preceding the Whist tricks).

In deciding what cards to play to the tricks, the player should consider, not only the value of the various combinations which he hopes to make (by reason of having parts of them in his hand), but the prospects of making them. Many players overlook this. Useful information on this point is to be found in the cards declared by the opponent.

If by chance a player held two Queens of Spades and a Jack of Diamonds, he would hold on to these as long as possible in the hope of making bezique, followed by double bezique. But if he sees his adversary declare a combination which includes the other Jack of Diamonds he knows at once that there is no hope of double bezique, and can play accordingly.

Again, two Aces in the hand appear to go a long way towards "four Aces". The prospect of drawing the other two is, however, very remote, and a player rather than hold them will do better to play and score them as brisques.

The following general maxims for play will also be found useful.

Do not take a trick unless you secure a brisque or wish to declare.

Observe carefully the cards which your opponent declares.

Reserve three or four trick-winning cards for the last three or four "stock" tricks.

Do not throw away cards which might later be useful, if you can help it. Sevens, eights, nines, and Jacks (except Jack of Diamonds) are the cards to throw away.

Do not be in too great a hurry to declare at the beginning of game, as this gives information to your opponent.

If you happen to hold one of the bezique cards, retain it as long as possible, even if you think there is little chance of making bezique. The uncertainty of its whereabouts will hinder your opponent.

Generally, a royal marriage should be declared early, and the cards retained as long as there is a chance of making sequence.

It is important to win the last of the stock tricks as this gives the lead for the Whist tricks. There are frequently several brisques to be made in these tricks. The leader to the first of these last eight tricks has the best chance of securing the majority of the brisques, because if equal cards are played to a trick (e.g. two Aces of trumps) the trick is won by the *leader*.

Brisques in reality are worth twenty each, viz. ten more for you, ten less for your opponent.

If your hand consists mainly of odd cards, Kings and Queens are the best to retain, because they form part of several combinations, viz. marriages, common and royal; four Kings, four Queens, bezique, and sequence.

If you have double bezique in your hand, undeclared, remember that bezique should be declared first, then double bezique.

Generally speaking, it is better to use cards that have been declared when playing to tricks, rather than those still in the hand. Your opponent thus receives less information. Of course cards exposed should not be played whilst there is still a chance of their making part of a new combination.

There are variations of Bezique wherein no card is turned up for trumps—the trump suit being decided by the first marriage declared, which is, therefore, a royal marriage.

Also, some players make the ten revert to its ordinary rank during the Whist tricks: this does not seem to be any improvement.

Again, there is diversity of opinion as to which is the "last" trick (for which ten points are scored). According to some it is the last of the "stock" tricks.

Such points should be agreed upon before play commences. Although Bezique is a very old game, there is no standard set of rules, and, therefore, no player should consider that *his* method is necessarily the right one.

Three-handed Bezique is played with three Piquet packs (ninety-six cards in all).

Triple bezique becomes possible, and is scored 1,000 or 1,500 points, the score for "game" usually being 2,000.

The play is exactly similar to that of the single-handed game, the order of playing to tricks being clockwise, as at Whist, etc.

The four-handed game may be played cut-throat (i.e. each against the rest) or by partners who sit alternately round the table.

Four packs are used, and consequently both triple and quadruple bezique may be scored. The latter is extremely rare, and is awarded from 1,500 to 3,000 points, according to the "game" score, which varies from 2,000 to 5,000 points. Triple bezique counts, as in the three-handed game, 1,000 to 1,500.

Combinations may be declared by a player partly by means of his own cards, and partly of cards of his partner, so long as the latter remain upon the table as part of some previously declared combination. Thus one player declaring a royal marriage, his partner may, after a further trick has been won by his side, add the Ace, ten, and Jack of trumps and declare sequence; or if four Kings have been declared by one player, his partner, adding the necessary Queens, may declare marriages with any or all of them. A player may declare after a trick taken either by himself or his partner, and it is lawful to inquire, before playing, whether one's partner has any declaration to make.

COMMERCE

THIS is really a very simple form of Poker, and is included
here mainly to serve as an introduction to games of the
Poker type, which are essentially different from the trick-
taking games in that there is no "play of the hand" in the
ordinary sense of the words. Commerce is, however, quite
a good game, notwithstanding its simplicity.

A fifty-two card pack is used, and players may number
from two up to seven, or even more.

Before the deal each player contributes an agreed stake
to the pool.

Three cards are dealt to each player. Each then inspects
his hand. The objects of the game are to secure one of the
following combinations: —

   (1) "Threes" (or pair-royal), viz. three cards of equal
       rank, such as three Queens.
   (2) "Sequence", viz. three cards of *the same suit* run-
       ning consecutively, such as four, five, six, or Jack,
       Queen, King.
   (3) "A point", viz. two or three cards of the same suit,
       the values of which added together make a high
       number. Ace counts as eleven, and court cards as
       ten each.

The first-named is the most valuable combination and
the last the least valuable.

In "threes" three Aces is better than three Kings and
so on. In "sequence" the higher sequence is the best,
i.e. Ace-King-Queen beats King-Queen-Jack, and so on.
Ace may also be counted as "one" in a sequence of one-
two-three.

In "points" the comparisons are simple, but a "point"
made with three cards is better than a "point" of the
same number made with two, e.g. Ace and King of, say,
Hearts, make a point of twenty-one, which would be
beaten by a point of twenty-one made by means of Jack,
seven and four of, say, Clubs.

After the deal the eldest hand, in order to improve his
cards, may either (1) "trade" or (2) "barter". If he wishes
to "trade" he pays one stake to the dealer (who keeps it)
at the same time discarding one of his own cards. The

dealer in exchange deals him another card (face down) from the pack.

If he wishes to "barter" he offers his unwanted card to the player on his left, who may take it and give a card he himself does not want in exchange. The player on the left may refuse to barter, but if he does so he must signify either by knocking on the table or saying "content" that he is satisfied with the cards he has. If he does this the hand is over, the cards are shown, and the best hand takes the pool.

More often of course the "trading" and "bartering" goes on for some time before anyone "knocks". It should be noted that each player in turn when he is dealer gets a little revenue from "trade". The advantage of trade (which costs a stake) over barter (which is free) is that in the latter your left-hand neighbour naturally gives you the worst card in his hand, and it is only a slender chance that it will prove of use to you.

There is another variety of the game, more nearly approaching one form of Poker, in which an extra hand called "the Widow", is dealt face up on the table. The eldest hand may exchange his whole hand for this if he likes. If he does not, each player in turn may exchange *one* card from his hand for one from the "widow". This goes on until someone "knocks", and cards are then shown and the highest hand wins the pool. If the eldest hand takes the widow complete on his first "say", the hands are shown at once. No player who has once declined to exchange can do so in a subsequent round.

BRAG

THIS game resembles Commerce to some extent, but more closely resembles true Poker. As in all "Poker" games there is no standard set of rules, and the variations of the game are almost innumerable. They all conform, however, to one main principle, in that the values of various hands are reckoned according to the comparative frequency with which certain combinations of cards are met with when dealt round in the usual way from a shuffled pack.

It will be appreciated that in a hand of three cards three Aces are very rarely found. This being so, three Aces is an extremely valuable hand in Brag. Other combinations are valued according to their rarity or otherwise.

The play consists in betting that your hand is better than your opponents', and if none of them is willing to take your bet, the cards are not shown at all. This of course rarely happens; there will almost always be someone to take a sporting chance.

Three cards make a "hand" at Brag. It is agreed beforehand whether three cards only shall be dealt to each player, or whether each shall have five dealt, two of which are discarded before play commences. The latter method makes the best game.

The hands rank in the following order of value: —

(1) *Three of a kind,* sometimes called "pair-royal", or "triplet". Three Aces of course beats three Kings; and so on.

(2) *Running flush,* i.e. three cards of the same suit in numerical order, Ace, King, Queen, beats King, Queen, Jack; and so on.

(3) A run, i.e. three cards of any suit in numerical order, Four, five, six, beats three, four, five; and so on.

(4) *A flush,* i.e. three cards of the same suit, in any order. The highest card of a flush determines its value compared with other flushes. Thus, a flush containing an Ace beats one containing lower cards. If the highest cards in two flushes are of the same value the next highest card is referred to.

(5) *A pair,* i.e. two cards of equal rank, as two Queens, two fives, of any suits. A pair of tens beats a pair of nines, and so on.

Note that all hands coming into one of the groups numbered above beat all hands coming into a lower group, e.g. the smallest run will beat the biggest of flushes.

Having learnt these values we will commence play.

The player on the dealer's left has first bet. He bets whatever he likes, subject to the "limit" (or nothing at all—in which case he says, "I drop out"), that his hand is better than anyone else's. If it is a valuable hand he will bet fairly high. But not too high, or he may get no takers. Let us suppose he bets threepence. The next player may "come in" if he thinks his hand is as good as the first player's. The first player having placed his stake in the pool, those that "come in" must each place a like amount.

But the third player may be confident that he holds the better hand; if so, he may "raise" the stakes, saying, "I raise it to sixpence."

If he does so, all those who "come in" after him must stake an equal amount.

The "raising" will probably cause the fourth or fifth player, who perhaps has a weak hand, to say, "I drop out". The turn thus comes round to the original caller again. If he is still confident that he holds the highest hand he may say, "I raise another threepence," paying *sixpence* into the pool. If, on the other hand, he is not so sure, he may pay threepence to make his stake equivalent to the third player's. This is called paying "to see". If this happens the hand is at an end. Those that have "come in", and remained in, will show their hands, he who has the highest taking the pool.

But the call may go round several times if someone "raises" during each round. Those wishing to remain in the game must make their stakes equivalent to the raiser's, or else make a further raise. Often all players but two drop out, and the hand ends by one player making his stake up to that of the raiser in order "to see" the "showdown", as it is called.

At first sight it may seem that success is a matter of pure chance. Not so; a good player will keep in mind the probabilities as to whether his hand is likely to have a serious rival, according as there may be few or many players. As explained in the section devoted to "Nap", and as all Nap players well know, if only half the pack is in use then it will be, roughly speaking, about even chances as to whether a given card is in play or not.

Further, the good player will save, and on occasion make money, by careful study of his opponents. There are many people who cannot conceal the fact that they have good cards, or vice versa. Their behaviour will vary of course in different individual cases. But by watching them certain useful indications will make themselves apparent.

On the other hand, a skilful player will cultivate methods of misleading his opponents, who, it must be remembered, are watching him for "signs" as to the real value of the hand on which he is betting.

The game may be played with the addition of the joker or "mistigris". This card can be counted as any card

FIG. 11.—The "Braggers"

in the pack, but hands which include it are inferior to "natural" hands, i.e. two Hearts and the joker count as a flush, but may be beaten by three "natural" (real) Hearts, even if they are of lower denomination.

In another form of the game the Ace of Diamonds, Jack of Clubs, and nine of Diamonds are all used as "jokers", and are called the "braggers".

Again, sometimes the dealer opens the game by putting up a stake (called the "ante") before the deal. All players must either "pay to see" or "raise", or else drop out.

It is impossible to note more than these variations, which emphasize the point that players should always agree to the method of play and betting before they commence.

POKER

In popular estimation Poker is a great "gambling" game. It is so "in law" also. Actually it is a game of pure science, and entails more skill and judgment than any other card game. The skill required is mathematical, and the judgment that of character.

The game probably possesses more variations than any other. So much so, that before commencing play it is necessary and a usual thing first to discuss exactly how the game shall be played. "Draw Poker" is the most commonly played variation, followed probably by what is known as "Whiskey Poker". But even these variations may be played in different ways, so that no player need consider that the variation with which he is familiar is "correct" or necessarily the best way of playing.

The hands are valued in the same manner as at Brag. But as a "hand" is five cards there are more possible combinations, and they run in slightly different order of value. The hands are: —

(1) *Straight flush*, i.e. running flush of five cards.

(2) *Fours*, i.e. four of the same value, as four Aces, which make the highest "four".

(3) *Full house* (or "Full hand"), i.e. a pair-royal and a pair. The pair-royal decides the winner as between two "full houses".

(4) *A flush*. Five cards of the same suit. The highest card or cards decide between two flushes.

(5) *A straight*. Five cards in numerical order, of any suits. Ace may be counted as high or low, i.e. as a "one" or as an Ace.

(6) *Threes*. A pair-royal, as three sixes.

(7) *Two pairs*. The highest pair decides between two or more hands of this type.

(8) *A pair*. Two cards of same value, a high pair beating a low pair.

If two or more hands should be equal as regards the main cards—as, for instance, two hands of two pairs, sixes, and sevens—then the odd card becomes the deciding factor. This principle applies throughout. If two hands are exactly equal, the pool is divided. Some players give value to the suits, and in this method no two hands can be equal.

The joker may be used if desired. Expert players consider that it does not improve the game, as it brings in too great an element of chance. If used, it may be counted as any card in the whole pack by the player fortunate enough to receive it. The highest hand when the joker is in use is five Aces. "Natural" hands are sometimes considered better than equivalent hands, including the joker. This is a point for agreement amongst the players.

Draw Poker is usually played as follows: —

Five cards are dealt to each player. Five players make the best game, but from three to seven may play. After the deal—for the privilege of which the dealer usually contributes one stake (called the "ante") to the pool—each player in turn is allowed, on payment of a stake into the pool, to receive additional cards up to five in number, discarding before he takes them from the dealer a like number from his original hand.

The dealer gives himself his own "draw" cards, but he must announce how many he is taking, so that all players can hear.

It will be seen that hands may be vastly improved by "drawing". If on the first deal you receive a pair and three indifferent cards, you will normally discard the latter and draw three more in the hope of turning the "pair" into a "three".

But the "draw" is more useful than this. By watching how many cards each player takes, you may receive a fair indication of what he commenced his hand with. It is, for example, tolerably certain that a player who draws three cards already holds a pair. His subsequent mien may indicate whether he has "improved" or not. Again, a player who draws one card may have either "fours" or the "makings" of a "flush", or a "straight", or even possibly of a "straight flush"; or he may have two pairs—which are the "makings" of a "full house".

Hence, beware of the player who draws one card, and observe him closely. He either has a very good hand, or one that is worthless or nearly so. If he bets cautiously, he probably has obtained the card he needed and wants as many players as possible to "come in". If he bets fiercely, he is perhaps "bluffing"—trying to make you think he "has them" by a display of confidence. There is an old Poker maxim which says, "Always see, but never raise, a one-card buy".

After all players have "drawn" (and you have duly noted each one), the player on the dealer's left may bet or "open", as it is called. If he does not desire to do so, the privilege passes to the next; and so on. Betting is usually as described for "Brag"; but there are many variations, some of which are rather complicated. The method should be agreed before play commences.

"Chips" (i.e. counters) are generally used instead of

actual money, being purchased (and subsequently "cashed") for so much a hundred from one of the players who acts as banker. As an example of how the betting goes, let us suppose that five players, A, B, C, D, and E, have all paid the necessary "ante" into the pool and drawn the cards they require. A has first call.

A: "I bet one" (puts up one "chip").

B: "I see one" (puts up one).

C: "I see and raise five" (puts up six).

D: "I see six" (puts up six).

E: "I see and raise ten" (puts up sixteen).

A: "I pass" (throws his hand to centre of table, unexposed).

B: "I see sixteen" (puts up fifteen, making sixteen with the one already betted).

C: "I retire" (throws in his cards).

D: "I see and raise ten" (puts up another twenty, making twenty-six, viz. six of his first bet, ten to see E's raise, and a further ten his own raise bet).

E: "I see" (puts in another ten).

B: "I see" (puts in another ten).

D: Shows his hand (all five cards) and says "three Aces".

E: "Beats me" (throws away his cards without showing them).

B: "I have a flush" (shows it and takes the pool).

(Had B not been able to beat three Aces he would have thrown away his cards without exposing them.)

It is usual to fix a "limit" before play commences. The limit is the largest amount that a player may bet at one time. It is also usually agreed that the "ante" (which indicates the smallest amount a player may bet) shall be a certain proportion of the limit—one-tenth, or one-twentieth.

By some players betting is indulged in *before the draw*. That is to say, a player may raise the amount necessary to "come in" (and draw cards), on the strength of the cards originally dealt to him. This has the effect of frightening out those who have been dealt weak hands at the outset.

The reader will have gathered that "bluffing" is a great part of the game. It is done in many ways other than the naïve scheme of plunging heavily on a hand worth nothing.

You may bluff your opponents by drawing only one

card when you hold, say, a "three". They will think you
hold "two pairs" or a "broken" straight or flush. In these
circumstances you stand a chance of a brisk contest with
an individual who holds two high pairs, who has decided
that you did not "improve", and that his pairs will beat
yours anyway.

Your "threes" will of course cause him to lose heavily
if he is a very positive sort of person.

Even if you attempt to bluff on nothing, and get found
out, it is not all dead loss. A little later on, when you
really have a good hand, you will find, perhaps, that a
larger number than usual of your opponents will "pay to
see" your hand, because they think you may be bluffing
again. Conversely, if you have had a succession of really
good hands and have won several "pots"—then a "bluff"
in the nature of a good hearty bet will often scare all the
others "out"—and you scoop the pool.

It may be noted again here that unless someone "pays
to see" your hand, he has no right to see it, and you should
not show it.

A few hints on general play: —

Always pay your stake and "draw", so long as you have
a pair of eights or higher in the original deal.

Do not pay to draw if your hand is merely mixed,
worthless cards. Above all, don't waste money on drawing
five cards, or four "to an ace". The odds are enormously
against your success. Avoid betting on "two pairs"; to
new players, especially if the pairs are "picture cards",
the hand looks good. It is practically worthless unless
there are only three players.

A "four straight flush with two openings" (or "open
both ends") by which is meant four cards of the same suit
running in order, to which you may draw a card, either at
the lower or higher end, is the best hand to draw cards to:
e.g. nine, ten, Jack, Queen of, say, Hearts; an eight or
King of Hearts will make a straight flush; any eight or
King will make a straight; any Heart will make a flush.

It is worth noting that, roughly speaking, the odds
against "improving" various incomplete hands are as
follows: —

A four straight flush (two openings) to a straight
   flush .   .   .   .   23 to 1
A four straight flush to simple flush .   .   .   4 to 1

D

A four straight flush to simple straight . . 5 to 1
(or, say, seven to four against any improvement).

Against filling a straight with one opening (e.g.
Ace, King, Queen, Jack, ten; or nine, eight,
seven, ten, five, etc.) . . . . . 11 to 1

Against filling a straight with two openings . 5 to 1

Against filling a flush . . . . . 4 to 1

Against improving one pair to two pairs . . 5 to 1

Against improving one pair to threes . . 7 to 1

Against improving one pair to a full . . . 98 to 1

Against improving one pair to fours . . 359 to 1
(or, say, 2½ to 1 against any improvements of
one pair).

FIG. 12.—A hand at Poker which "looks
good," but is not

(It will be noted that the best odds are those in respect
of filling a flush. But this is counteracted by the fact that
the odds against getting four cards of the same suit in the
original deal are fairly long.)

Against improving two pairs to a full . . 11 to 1

Against improving threes to a full . . . 15 to 1

Against improving threes to fours . . . 23 to 1
(or, say, 8½ to 1 against any improvement of
threes).

It is on the comparison of these odds, coupled with
careful observations of other players' methods of drawing,
that the good Poker player bases his betting.

Remember always to watch what your opponents draw, and their subsequent behaviour. It is on this that success largely depends.

Do not get into habits, e.g. of bluffing when you are winning lots of money, or when you have lost a lot. It will soon be noticed, and you will suffer.

On the other hand, watch for such habits on the part of other players; you may be able to profit by it.

Because you have lost one chip to the pot is no justification for losing two. Money is made at Poker by saving it.

The expert Poker player earns no reputation for anything, save that he is a good player; i.e. he is not noted as either timid, bold, careless, cautious, or as a "bluffer"

FIG. 13.—A hand, not so good looking,
that will beat it easily

There is no standard code of laws for Poker. Those generally accepted and given by the best authorities are as under:—

(1) The cards must be shuffled by the player on the dealer's left and cut by the player on his right.

(2) The cards must be dealt one at a time.

(3) If two cards are turned up in a deal, there must be a new deal. It is an old established custom that one card turned up in a deal must be accepted.

(4) Each player, including the dealer, must announce in a sufficiently loud voice for everyone to hear how many cards he draws, or if he draws none.

(5) No player after he has been given the number of cards asked for can be called upon to name the number.

(6) Each player must discard, and throw to the centre of the table, face downwards, the number of cards he wishes to exchange before drawing the required number of cards. The discard may not be looked at afterwards.

(7) If a card is exposed in the draw, the player cannot accept that card. He takes those not exposed, and after all the other players have made their draw, another card is given in place of the exposed card.

(8) The bottom card of the pack may not be given in the draw.

(9) If there are not sufficient cards in the stock to complete a draw, the number there are, less the bottom card, are taken, the balance being given from the other players' discards, which shall be shuffled.

(10) No player may declare to come in, bet, see or raise out of his turn. Nor may a player throw up his hand out of turn either on the "come in" or after the draw. But players not coming in, or not betting, seeing, or raising, shall immediately throw their cards to the centre of table when their turn to speak comes round.

(11) The dealer is responsible for the pot; he must ask each player in his turn if he comes in, and if so see that the player "tits up" correctly; he is responsible that the bets are made in correct order, and that all chips for bets, raises, and calling are duly put up by the players concerned. The dealer, in fact, rules the table for his deal.

(12) If a player having been dealt six cards picks them up, he cannot play on that hand (unless he comes in and draws five cards). But if he does not pick them up, he can call upon the dealer to take back one of the cards, and the hand is good. If a player be dealt and picks up four cards, he may call on the dealer to give him a fifth card, and the hand is good.

(13) If a player, after the draw, finds he has more than five cards he cannot win the pot under any circumstances even though he bets and is not seen. The pot in this latter case is left and replayed for. But a player holding less than five cards can win the pot if his bet is seen, and it is discovered he has less than five cards.

(14) If a player be given more cards than he has asked for, he can call upon the dealer to rectify the error, provided he has not picked up any of the cards so given him. If he has been given too few cards, the error can be rectified any time before the betting begins.

EUCHRE

THIS is an American game, which, possibly, accounts for its somewhat curious phraseology. At first acquaintance it appears simple; but it requires quite as much skill to play as Napoleon (which it resembles to some extent) or possibly more.

It may be played by two, three, or four players. A Piquet pack (i.e. an ordinary pack minus the cards from two to six inclusive) plus a joker, is used. The cards rank in the usual order, except that the joker is counted as the highest trump; the *Jack* of the trump suit is the second best trump, and the Jack of the *other suit of the same colour* is third best. After these come the trumps in proper order, viz. Ace, King, Queen, ten, etc. The two Jacks mentioned have peculiar names: the Jack of the trump suit is called the "right bower", and the Jack of the suit of corresponding colour is called the "left bower". When the left bower is led, players must follow suit with a card of the trump suit.

The actual play of the hand is exactly as at Nap, except that there are now three extra trumps above the ace. A game is five points. The objects of the game are to make three or five tricks in a hand. Making four tricks has no advantage over making three. Three tricks, called a "point", count one point. Five tricks are called a "march" and score two points. A player who fails to make at least a point is said to be "euchred", and his opponent scores two points.

The peculiarities of the game are in the preliminaries before the play of the hand.

Five cards are dealt to each player, usually by twos and threes, and the next card is turned up on the top of the pack as trump card.

For the sake of clearness we will describe the two-handed game first.

The non-dealer has first "say"; and if, after inspecting his hand, he thinks he can make a "point" (three tricks) with the suit turned up as trumps, he says, "I order it up". This means that he orders the dealer to take the trump card up into his hand. The dealer does not do this until after the first card has been led; but immediately the order is given he discards one of his own cards, placing it underneath the pack. If, however, the non-dealer does not think he can make three tricks, he says, "I pass".

FIG. 14.—The six best trumps at Euchre
Diamonds being trumps

It is now the dealer's turn, and he considers whether or not he can make a point. If he thinks he can, he says, "I take it up"; and places his discard under the pack in readiness to do so. If, however, he does not think so, he says, "I turn it down", and does so, by putting the *trump card* underneath the pack.

The non-dealer may now decide which suit shall be trumps, and he may say, "I make it Clubs", or Hearts, or whatever will best suit him. In doing this it must be understood that he is declaring to make at least three tricks.

If he does not think he can make three tricks, even when naming his own trumps, he again says, "I pass". Whereupon the dealer, if it suits him, may "make it" any suit he pleases. If he, too, passes the hand is thrown in and a new deal made.

The trump suit having been settled, the non-dealer leads: the dealer (after picking up the trump card, if it has not been "turned down") plays to the trick in the ordinary way and wins it if he can. The trick winner has the lead to the next trick, and the hand is played out in the usual way.

In the three-handed game, the procedure is the same. The elder hand or the next player may pass or "order", the dealer to take up the trump. If they both pass, the dealer may, "take it up" or "turn it down". If he turns it down, the elder hand and then the others in succession may now "make it" what they wish—or pass.

Scoring in the three-handed game is slightly different. If the challenger (i.e. he who "orders it", "takes it", or "makes it") fails to make at least a point, the other two players do not each score two points, because this might have the effect of bringing them both to "game" at the same time. The two points are *deducted* from the score of the challenger. If he has no score, he is considered to be *minus* two. Which means that he must take seven for game.

Four players play as partners, two against two, sitting alternately. The "calling" is as before described, except that the dealer's partner, who has second call, does not say, "I take it up" but "I assist". This means that he is confident that, with his cards, and the trump card taken into the dealer's hand, they can make the three tricks necessary for a point. When dealer's partner "assists" the third and fourth players do not call. The dealer discards at once, and after the first lead takes up the trump card. If the second player passes, third player may "order it up" or pass; if he passes the dealer may "take it up" or pass. If all have passed the call goes round a second time, each player in turn having the option of "making it" what he likes, in his proper turn. When the trump suit is "made", play proceeds on the lines of Whist. The procedure outlined may be varied by a player deciding to *play alone*. In this case, when his turn comes to call, he must say, "I play alone". This is equivalent to "ordering it up" or "taking it up", according to whether he is on the dealing or non-dealing side. His partner lays his cards face down on the table and takes no further part in the hand.

The "lone hand", as he is called, plays against the other two—and has the advantage that if he scores a "march" he gets *four* points instead of two for his side. A point, however, scores only one, as usual, or two to his opponents if he is euchred.

Another peculiarity of Euchre is the method of marking the score. Each player (or partnership) has two of the spare cards from the pack—a three and a four—and the method is as follows: —

The three face upwards with the four turned face down upon it (as in Fig. 15) indicates "one". It does not matter how much of the three is exposed. The four face upwards with the three turned face down upon it indicates "two" (see Fig. 16). The three completely exposed with the four

FIG. 15.—A score of one as marked at Euchre

FIG. 16.—A score of two as marked at Euchre

underneath means "three" (Fig. 17), whilst the four similarly exposed indicates "four" (Fig. 18).

The following hints on playing will be useful to beginners: —

In view of the fact that a point of three tricks successfully made counts only one point, whilst an unsuccessful attempt gives the other side two points, it is obvious that to "order it up" requires a hand containing three practically certain tricks.

Normally, without such a hand, you should pass. If, however, the score stands at four all, and you are on the non-dealing side and have a fair number of trumps with nothing better in other suits, it is advisable to risk "ordering it", even though you are not certain of three tricks; the reason being that if dealer or his partner accepts the turned-up trump you are no worse off, whilst if they "make it" another suit you are practically bound to lose. Hence you have only one chance to make game, viz. to play the hand with trumps according to the turn up, because they are the best you can get.

In the four-handed game, the elder hand should not, however, order it up invariably when he has a strong hand. It should be remembered that it pays better to euchre your opponents than to make a point yourself. Hence if you hold *both* bowers, a fairly high trump and good cards in

FIG. 17.—A score of three as marked at Euchre

FIG. 18.—A score of four as marked at Euchre

the suit corresponding in colour to the trump (called the "next" suit) it is advisable to pass. If your opponents "take it up" you can probably euchre them and score two points: if they "turn it down" you can "make it next" (i.e. make trumps the other suit of same colour) and, still having good trumps and two bowers, make your point fairly easily, even if you cannot play "alone", make a "march", and score four.

It is generally considered that a player may "assist" on a hand somewhat weaker than that required to "order it up". The theory is that, the elder hand having passed, he has admitted weakness in the trump suit turned up. This is not necessarily so: he may be lying low for the reasons indicated in the preceding paragraph. Hence a player should not attempt to make his calls by hard and fast rules.

The state of the score is always an important consideration, wherever you may happen to be playing. If your opponents are three up, a euchre will make them game, therefore be cautious. It is generally considered that three fair trumps with an Ace of another suit will make a point, but with the score at three all, it would be sound play to pass unless the three trumps were high.

On the advisability of "turning it down" the state of the score again has important bearings. If your score is well ahead of your opponents, you may do so without much risk of their getting game with trumps of their own making. If, however, they only require one for game, it is better to "take it up" on any sort of hand that has a chance of making a point.

If the trump is turned down, the next player should, usually, "make it next", if he can, because it is unlikely that your opponents would have turned it down if either of them held one of the bowers. Hence you know your opponents are to some extent weak in the "next suit" (being minus the bowers) whereas in the "cross" suits (opposite colours) for all you know they may have both the bowers.

For similar reasons the dealer's partner, or dealer, if it is left to either of them, should "make it across" (i.e. make a suit of opposite colour trumps), because each should know that his partner, having passed or turned down the original trump, is therefore likely to be weak in suits of that colour.

From the foregoing it will be seen that the use of the "Jack of the same colour" as third best trump is more than a mere freak of fancy. It establishes a connection between two suits and has an important influence on play, for the reason that the two Jacks of the trump colour are second and third best trumps, or vice versa, whichever of the suits in question is finally decided upon.

There is one situation in Euchre which, for some obscure reason, is known as "the bridge". It is when the score of the dealing side is one and that of the non-dealers four. In these circumstances it is a convention that, with weak cards, the elder hand should always order it up. The weaker his cards the more urgent is the necessity to do so.

The idea is to prevent the possibility of your opponents, the dealers, from playing "alone" and possibly scoring four and making "game". The theory will be found to be quite sound in the long run; if you "order it up" and are euchred your opponents score only two and there is still a chance for you to make game in the next hand.

The right bower, or the left bower and another trump,

are sufficient to prevent a "lone hand" scoring a march and game. Hence if you hold either of these you need not "order it up" unless it suits you to do so. If your opponents take it up you can possibly euchre them. And anyway you will be no worse off. If the call comes to your partner, he will know from the fact of your not ordering it up that your hand is not very weak; and he can, therefore, afford to order it up on a quite moderate hand. If he is so weak that he cannot, and the dealer takes it up, you are still no worse off. Whilst if the dealer turns it down, you can "make it next" with every prospect of securing the point and game.

The following brief notes comprise the main principles of sound play: —

If you cannot follow suit or trump, throw away your weakest card.

When second player, if compelled to follow suit, win the trick, if possible.

When playing second, do not trump a small card the first time round, but leave it to your partner. Throw away any single card lower than an Ace, so that you may afterwards trump the suit you throw away.

When third player, trump with high or medium trumps so as to force the high trumps of the dealer.

If your partner "assists", and you hold a card next higher than the turn-up card, trump with it when an opportunity occurs.

If your partner has "assisted", and has played a trump, and you have won a trick and the lead, do not lead him a trump unless you hold commanding cards. Your partner may have assisted on two trumps only, in which case such a lead would draw his remaining trump.

When your partner leads the Ace of a plain suit, and you have none, do not trump it; if you have a single card, discard that.

When you make the trump "next" in suit, always lead a trump.

When you hold two trumps, two cards of one plain suit, and a single card of another suit, lead one of the two plain cards.

If you hold three small trumps, and good plain cards, and desire to euchre your opponents, lead a trump; for when trumps are exhausted you may make your commanding plain suit cards.

If you have lost the first two tricks and won the third, and you hold a trump and a plain card, play the former. It is your only chance to make or save a euchre.

When your partner has made or adopted the trump it is bad play to win the lead, unless you possess a hand sufficiently strong to play for a march.

If the game stands three all, think before you adopt or make a trump upon a weak hand, for a euchre will make your adversaries "game".

When you are one and your opponents have scored four, you may risk trying to make it "alone" upon a weaker hand than if the score was more favourable to you.

When you are elder hand, and the score stands four for you, and one for your opponents, always order up the trump, to prevent either of them from going "alone". You need not do this, however, if you hold the right bower, or the left bower and another trump.

Always "make it next", if possible, when you are on the non-dealing side; but "make it across", if possible, when you are on the dealing side.

And, finally, never lose sight of the state of the score, nor forget to make your calls accordingly.

FARO

FARO is a very exciting game in which a good deal of skill may be exercised, not, however, in playing the cards, but in determining the likely possibilities of their appearance. The only objection to the game is that it lends itself to gambling; but this need be no deterrent, if people play for small stakes or use counters.

Faro requires a certain amount of apparatus; but this may be either fashioned at home, or done without. The first requisite is a "lay-out". This consists of a green cloth, large enough to cover the table. In the middle of the cloth, a full set of spades is painted, or the cards may be taken from a spare pack and sewn on. The suit is arranged in two rows, thus: In the first row, to the left, is the King, followed by the Queen, the Jack, the ten, the nine and

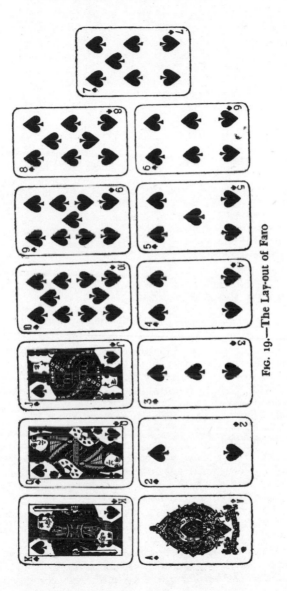

FIG. 19.—The Lay-out of Faro

the eight. In the second row, below the King, is the Ace, below the Queen is the two, and this is followed by the three, four, five and six. The seven is placed at the right-hand end of the two rows, on a line of its own, midway between the other rows.

In addition, a specially constructed box is needed. It is just large enough to contain a full pack and it operates in the following manner: the dealer shuffles the cards and puts them in the box, from below, and then closes the door. He puts them in face upwards and, thus, the top card can be seen; but it cannot be moved unofficially, because the opening is smaller than a card. When play is about to begin, the dealer pulls a handle and the top card shoots out of the box, through a slit in the side. Springs, arranged at the bottom of the box, press the remaining cards up to the top and, thus, one card can be always ejected, as long as any remain, by the simple operation of pulling the handle. Obviously, the only virtue in using the box is to prevent any tampering with the pack, once it has been made. It is equally obvious that when a game is played among friends a simple pack, without any box, can serve the same purpose.

The banker or dealer sits at the table facing the "lay-out" and an assistant usually takes up a position beside or opposite to him. The players stand round or sit where they choose. A pack of fifty-two cards is shuffled and placed in the box, already described, and the door or lid is closed. Perhaps it should be said that the thirteen cards forming the "lay-out" are not taken from the playing pack; they are entirely separate.

The game consists in staking on the cards that are likely to turn up or, more correctly speaking, which may chance to be thrown out of the box. This is how they are played: When all the staking is complete, the banker throws the top card out of the box and, as it has been seen by everybody, it does not count.

The top card being ejected, it uncovers another card, and this is taken by the banker himself. As it is his card, he appropriates all the money or counters staked on it in the "lay-out". It must be said that only the value of a card is considered in Faro and not the suit.

Next, the banker ejects his card from the box and uncovers another. This card is the property of the players and the banker pays out to all those who have staked on the card that has happened to turn up.

These two cards constitute a "turn", and those who have staked on cards other than the two that happened to turn up, reclaim their bets, neither winning nor losing.

The game continues, turn after turn, with fresh stakes each time, until the whole pack has been used. Certain variations are permitted in staking when the pack is nearing the end; these will be discussed later.

From this description, it may be thought that Faro is nothing more than a game of blind betting. In actuality, it is far from such a thing. During the first few turns, it may be little more than a game of chance; but, after that, it needs very skilful reckoning to be able to surmise what may and what cannot turn up.

Obviously, the things that are likely to happen depend very considerably on what has happened and, so that a player may be able to keep a score of what has gone before, he provides himself with a little chart on which is printed a list of the thirteen different cards. As a card turns up, he marks his list and, when one particular card has appeared four times, the player knows it is useless to bank on it; when it has appeared three times, it may but is not likely to come up, and so on.

As far as we have described the game, it would appear that the banker has no better chance of winning than a player; but this, of course, is contrary to human nature. The banker's advantage comes when a pair constitutes a turn. In other words, when both the cards of a turn are of like value, then the banker takes half the stakes.

Naturally, even this advantage can be very considerably negatived. Suppose, for instance, that three Kings have already turned up. The far-seeing player notes the fact and, then, stakes heavily on the king. He does this because he knows that, should he win, he will not have to halve the money, because it is impossible at this stage for two more Kings to appear.

In laying stakes, a coin or counter placed upon a card forming part of the "lay-out" is considered to be a bet on that card; if it is mid-way between two cards, it is a stake divided between the two cards; if it is mid-way between four cards, it refers to these four cards, and so on.

But it should be noted that local customs considerably affect these matters and a player should acquaint himself, beforehand, how stakes are to be laid, when playing in strange places.

TECHNICAL TERMS

The Hock is the last card remaining in the box, after the full deal of turns has been made. When one turn remains to be made, there are three cards in the box; they may be, for example, the six, seven and eight; we will suppose the last turn to be six and seven, leaving the eight in the box, which would be called the *hock* card, because, as the game was originally played, the dealer took "hock", that is, all the money which happened to be placed upon that card; the bank, therefore, had a certainty of winning that money, without the possibility of losing it—hence the term *hock,* which means *certainty.*

A Deal.—The dealer is said to have made a deal, when he has dealt out all the cards of the pack.

A Turn.—The two cards drawn from the dealer's box —one for the bank and the other for the player—constitute a *turn*.

Coppering a Bet.—If a player wishes to bet that a card will lose (that is, win for the bank), he signifies his wish, by placing a copper coin upon the top of his stake. It is called "coppering", because coppers were first used to distinguish such bets.

To Bar a Bet.—A player having a bet upon a card, and wishing to bar it for a turn, must say to the dealer, "I bar this bet for the turn," pointing to it, in which case it can neither lose nor win.

Last Call.—When three cards only remain in the box, any player has the privilege of calling the order in which they will be dealt—this is termed the last call. The checks are placed so as to express the call, and if correctly made, the bank pays four to one, and if a "cat", two for one.

A Cat or Cat Harpen.—When the last turn consists of two cards of the same denomination, and one other card, as two tens and a king, it is called a cat.

Paroli or Parlee.—Suppose a player to bet sixpence upon the Ace—it wins and the dealer pays it; if the player then allows the shilling to remain upon the Ace, he is said to play his *paroli*, which means, the original stake and all its winnings.

Pressing a Bet is to add to the original stake.

Repeating and Reversing.—A card is said to repeat when it plays as it did upon the previous deal, and to *reverse* when it plays directly opposite; that is, if it won four times, it is said to reverse if it loses four times.

Sleepers.—A bet is said to be a sleeper when the owner has forgotten it, when it becomes public property, anyone having a right to take it.

A Bet or Case Card.—When three cards of one denomination have been dealt, the one remaining in the box is called the *bet, case* or *single* card.

The Soda Card is the top card of the deck when put into the dealing-box, preparatory to a deal.

Playing a Bet Open is to bet a card will win, not to lose.

Betting Even Stakes is when the player constantly bets the same amount.

BLIND HOOKEY (Banker)

THIS game has considerable popularity in certain circles, and is a pure gamble.

There are various methods of play, but the essence of the game is simply to bet that a card you have received, by one method or another, is better than one received or retained by the dealer.

Any number up to nine may play. The dealer—who is the "banker"—is decided by cutting. He shuffles the cards (an ordinary pack) and has them cut by the player on his right. He then allows each player to cut a small number of cards (not less than four) from the top of the pack. Those that are left he retains. No player looks at his cards. Each places his stake beside his cards and the dealer then shows the bottom card of his packet. The other players do the same. The dealer pays out an amount equivalent to their stakes to all who have cards higher than his. All who have cards equal to his or lower lose their stakes to the dealer. If and when the dealer pays out to all players, the deal passes to the next player, and so on.

Instead of allowing each player to cut his own cards, the dealer may cut the pack into three parts. The players choose any two of them and leave the dealer the third. They place their stakes beside one or other of the packets chosen and the cards are turned up and stakes lost or won as before.

The only hint it is necessary to give on playing Banker is: Don't play with strangers!

SLIPPERY SAM

SLIPPERY SAM is quite similar to Blind Hookey or Banker, but many players consider it the better game.

Somebody offers himself or is otherwise chosen to become the banker. This individual allots a certain sum —it may be anything he likes—to constitute the bank; then, he shuffles the pack of fifty-two cards and the player on his right cuts. This done, the banker deals out three cards to each person and sets down the remainder of the pack, the top card of which is not seen.

The first player now looks at his hand and it is his duty to commence. He may do one of two things: (a) he may pass, in which case the next player on his left takes the turn, or (b) he may bet any sum he likes, as long as it does not exceed the amount in the bank, that he has a card in his hand which will beat the turn-up. Be it noted that, as yet, he has no notion as to what the turn-up is. Directly the bet is made, however, the banker turns up the top card and the player spreads out his hand.

In deciding whether there is anything in the hand to beat the turn-up, each card is valued exactly as it is in Whist, i.e. an Ace ranks highest and a two lowest. In addition, the card to beat the turn-up must be not only of a higher rank but of the same suit. There can be, of course, no trumps.

When the first bet is concluded, the cards concerned in it are thrown on one side and the turn-up goes, too. It is the turn, then, of the next player, who makes his bet in an exactly similar manner and, when he has decided on his course, a fresh card is turned up. So the game proceeds until every player has had an opportunity of making a bet.

There are very definite rules about the banker. The moment his bank is broken, he must withdraw and give the deal to someone else. If, however, he thrives, he cannot vacate his position until he has completed three deals. He *may* quit then; but he *must* go after four. During the course of the play, the banker is required to keep the money on the table, not in his hand, and any winnings must be added to the bank and nothing may be withdrawn except to pay out bets. The usual procedure is for the bank to pass round the table, working to the left.

Slippery Sam is one of the games beloved of cardsharpers, and it is good advice to warn players against taking a hand with people who are unknown. Apart from that, it is a game which provides very reasonable chances, since a punter sees his cards before he binds himself.

It must not be thought that the game is pure chance and nothing more. A quick head for figures and a facility for remembering the cards that have been played already will go far towards making a good player. The law of averages plays a big part, too.

When should a punter bet that he can beat the turn-up and when should he decline? These are questions which every player will be sure to ask. To answer this, we may set out a few figures. Suppose that a hand consists of three cards, all of which are tens. In the pack, there are the Jack, Queen, King and Ace of the suits shown by the tens and a complete additional suit to beat the hand; i.e., twenty-five cards in all. Similarly, in the pack there are the nine, eight, seven, six, five, four, three and two of three suits which the hand will beat; i.e. twenty-four cards in all. Therefore, a hand of something better than three tens is needed to win, according to the law of averages. Of course, allowances must be made for used-up cards, and it is here that skill will tell.

VINGT-UN (Pontoon)

PONTOON, as it is commonly called in this country, is the best known (to the average Englishman) of a very large family of games of chance which have for the central idea the objective of getting nearer to a given number (by means of card values added together) than one player who is for the time being the "banker".

As the name indicates, twenty-one is the number aimed at. An ordinary pack is used and any number may play. The dealer is the banker, and is chosen by any of the usual methods.

Having decided upon the dealer, the maximum stakes are agreed upon. Play begins as follows: The dealer gives one card to each player, and finally one to himself, face down. Each player may look at his card, including the dealer. Stakes are placed alongside the cards by each punter. The object of the game is to get cards which count twenty-one, or as near it as possible, *but not over it*. All court cards count ten, the Ace counts eleven or one, as desired by the holder. A player, or the dealer, therefore,

FIG. 20.—A "Natural" at Vingt-un

holding an Ace and a court card is said to have a "natural". Stakes are, however, "made" on the first card dealt. The dealer, if he receives a good first card, may say to the players, "I double you." This entitles the dealer to receive from each player double the amount of the stake in each case where the dealer wins; he also undertakes to pay out to the successful punters double the amount of their stake. The dealer wins on "evens" and on lower card combinations than his own, except in the case of a "natural" of two cards, which is provided for by cancellation.

After stakes have been made, and doubled or not, as the dealer decides, a second card is given to each in turn, the dealer getting his own last, still face downwards. Each player, including the dealer, inspects his cards. If the dealer finds that his two cards make a natural, he turns them up and declares this fact, and receives from each player *double* the amount of the stake (or four times its value if it has been doubled). If, however, one of the punters has also a "natural", he declares this and the two cancel each other.

But if the dealer, on inspecting his two cards, finds

that he had not a "natural", it is his duty to offer a card, or cards as may be required, to each player in turn. If either of them has a "natural" he declares it, and receives from the dealer twice his stake (or four times its value if it has been doubled). The third and subsequent cards to each player will be dealt face upwards. The dealer's turn comes last. The players need not take a card, nor need the dealer. For, although the game is almost purely one of chance, there are certain principles which will materially assist a player if he knows and uses them consistently.

If, for example, a punter found that he had a court card dealt for his first, and an eight or a nine for his second, he would "stand"—or decline a third. If a player accepts cards which make his total over twenty-one he is "over", and must pay up his stake and throw his cards to the centre of the table. With cards counting as above, eighteen or nineteen, the chances are that a further card accepted would make him "over", as there are many more cards of value above three or four than below. It is prudent, in fact, to "stand" at seventeen or even sixteen. The dealer is similarly guided.

When each player is satisfied to "stand", including the dealer, the latter "declares" his hand and receives from all players who are "even" or "under" his hand. To those over he pays the amount of their stakes. Should the dealer with his third card make twenty-one he receives from all players. After the stakes have been paid or received, the deal is continued for another round from the remaining cards, which are dealt with the exception of the last, which is always thrown face upwards on the table. The cards which have been used are gathered, shuffled, and cut, and handed to the dealer by another player when wanted to complete the deal. The deal passes to another player, or to each in succession, as may be arranged, either by a time limit, termination of the pack, or on the dealer being beaten all round by the punters.

A player drawing two Aces may decide to draw extra cards for each, announcing to the dealer, "I go on both."

There is a variation of the game wherein the deal passes only when a player gets a "natural", which is turned up at once and is paid for at three times the stake. Twenty-one is paid double, and the "run", i.e. five cards drawn without "bursting", is paid double. A player drawing two

similar cards can go on both, and two Aces (the lowest
hand in two cards) is paid *four* times the stake, but deal
does not pass. If two players obtain a natural, the first on
dealer's left only gets paid three times the stake and gets
deal; the other gets paid double simply as twenty-one. If
the dealer and player obtain "naturals", the dealer gets
paid single stakes from that player and keeps the deal. He
gets of course three times the stake from the other players.
The dealer cannot go for five cards without "breaking",
that is, the hand only counts its normal value with him.
If a player gets two Aces and dealer a natural, the player
gets single stakes.

The dealer has, it should be observed, much the best
position. He has the advantage of winning when there is
a tie, and is also able to "double" when he likes. He does
this when (1) he has a good card, and (2) the punters generally speaking do not seem to have good cards—judging
from their small stakes. Good players assert that with an
Ace or "ten" card as his first, he should always double
provided the stakes do not indicate many good cards
amongst the punters.

QUINZE

THIS game is very much like Vingt-un, but is designed for
two players only. The number aimed at is fifteen (Fr.:
quinze).

An ordinary pack is used and the plain cards have
their usual value, according to "pips", whilst the Ace
counts as one and all court cards as ten. The stake is
agreed beforehand, and the players cut for deal. Ace counts
low, and the lowest cut indicates the dealer. He deals one
card to his opponent and one to himself. The non-dealer
looks at his card, and if he wishes may draw one or more
cards in the hope of getting a total of fifteen, or near it,
but not over it. *After* he has drawn, or refused, the dealer
has a similar option, and draws cards if he wishes. When
both are content the cards are shown, and the player with
fifteen, or who is nearest to it, takes both stakes. If either
player overdraws (i.e. more than fifteen) he loses. If both
overdraw, stakes are doubled for the next deal.

Some players double the stakes next deal if there is a

tie; others agree that in such a case the dealer wins.

If you wish to win in the long run do not draw further cards unless your total is less than nine.

THIRTY-ONE

THIRTY-ONE is a game of the same genus as Vingt-un and Quinze, but it contains additional elements and is an improvement on both as a "family game".

An ordinary pack is used, and, as in Vingt-un, Aces count as eleven, and court cards as ten; other cards according to the number of their "pips".

Any number of players may take part. There is no banker, an agreed stake being paid by each player into the pool. The deal is decided in the usual way, and passes to each player in turn.

Three cards are dealt, one at a time, to each player, and an additional hand of three cards in the centre of the table. This extra hand is exposed before play commences. The elder hand first, and the others in the customary rotation, may each exchange one card from their hands for one of those in the extra hand. The discard is put in the place of the card taken—face upwards.

The object of the game is to make thirty-one, but the cards making it must be *all of the same suit*. Obviously the only cards possible are an Ace and two court cards or a ten.

The nearest hand to thirty-one is, however, three "of a kind" (pair-royal), and a player may try for this instead. It counts thirty and a half, and should more than one player secure it the highest pair-royal is the best (i.e. three Aces are better than three Kings, and so on). After "three of a kind" comes the highest total in any one suit.

The exchanging of cards goes on until some player is satisfied, which he signifies by knocking on the table or saying "content". It should be noted that a player *must* exchange or else "knock". He cannot knock immediately after an exchange, but must wait until his turn comes again.

When a player has knocked, the others may each make one more exchange if they wish. The hands are then shown, and the highest takes the pool.

BACCARAT

This game, in its two forms, Baccarat Banque and Baccarat Chemin de Fer, is the fashionable member of the Vingt-un family. It is very popular at public tables on the Continent.

The players are divided as usual into punters and a dealer. The dealer is decided upon in the first instance by putting the "bank" up to auction, the person who is prepared to risk the largest sum having the privilege. He must put the whole of the sum on the table before him. He may retire from the position of banker when he wishes, and is succeeded either by the next player in turn, if that player is willing to put up a sum equivalent to the last "bank", or the deal may be auctioned again.

The players sit on both sides of the dealer. Twenty constitute a full table. They may not bet collectively more than the bank which is before the dealer: the amount of this varies, as the dealer is bound to leave all his winnings in the "bank". The player immediately on the dealer's right bets first. He may bet the full amount of the bank, but usually does not. After he has bet the player on the dealer's immediate left may bet to the "uncovered" balance of the bank. Subsequently, the next player on the dealer's right, then the next player on the dealer's left, and so on, make their bets, each being limited by the balance remaining "uncovered" when his turn comes. If all the players together do not put up an amount equivalent to the bank, the dealer may remove the difference from his bank.

All bets are made before cards are dealt. From three to six packs of cards are used. Each player may shuffle in turn. The dealer deals the first card to the player on his right, the second to him on his left, and the third to himself. Then another to the right, one to the left and one to himself. All cards are dealt face down. When the deal is complete, the dealer first inspects his cards, and then the other two players do likewise.

It will be observed that although there may be twenty-one players, only the dealer and his two neighbours receive cards. Each of these two players represents all those who are seated on the same side. And his play is *on behalf of the side.* Consequently there are rigid conventions which he must observe.

Nine is the highest and winning score at Baccarat, eight being next best, and so on. The Ace counts as one, plain cards according to their pips, and court cards as tens. The tens are, however, ignored in reckoning the score. Thus a King and two are counted as *two* only. An Ace and six are reckoned as six. Nine and eight as seven; Queen and eight as eight. A score of ten or twenty is called "Baccarat" and is entirely ignored. It will be seen, therefore, that it is impossible to get *more* than nine.

If, upon inspection of the two cards dealt, the dealer or either of the players finds he holds a "natural" eight or nine he must turn his cards up and announce the fact at once. If the dealer has a natural, he wins all the stakes unless there is another natural, in which case he wins if he is the higher, loses if he is the lower. If the naturals are equal the bets on that side are "off".

When the dealer has not a natural he announces that he "gives". The two players may each in turn have *one* card, or they may "stand". After giving the cards required, face upwards, the dealer may also have one if he wishes. He then announces his score (or point as it is called) and the other players show theirs. The nearest to nine, as between dealer and punter, wins: equal scores cancel out.

As an illustration: Suppose the dealer is A, and the right and left players B and C. B receives in the deal a King and three, C receives four and two, and A a ten and five. The dealer would "give". B would draw one card, say an eight, making his score $10 + 3 + 8 = 1$ (the twenty being ignored). C should "stand" with the score of $4 + 2 = 6$. The dealer A may draw if he wishes: he would probably do so, and get, say, a three; making his score $10 + 5 + 3 = 8$. He would announce his "point" as 8, and the other players showing theirs as 1 and 6 respectively, he would receive all stakes.

The rigid convention mentioned above applies to the drawing of the extra card by the punter. If his point be six or seven, he will refuse. If it be less than five, he will accept. If it be five, he may accept or decline. Any other course of play, since his action influences the fate of the stakes of others, is against the recognised procedure. In some circles a breach of these principles is punished by a fine, or even by compelling the offender to pay up the stakes of the other players if they should be lost.

The hand being complete, the used cards are thrown into a waste basket. The deal is made, as before, from the unused cards, except that if either or both of the players seated next to the dealer has lost in the previous deals, the cards are dealt to the next player in rotation. The deal is to the same player as long as he wins for his side, but passes to the next as soon as he loses.

There are certain odds in favour of the dealer at Baccarat (computed to be about $7\frac{1}{2}$ per cent) and this arises from the fact that the dealer does not make his decision as to "drawing" until he has seen the cards drawn by the players. He of course knows the conventions, and if a player does not draw he therefore knows his point is either 5, 6, or 7. If the player does draw he knows his point was (before the draw) either 0, 1, 2, 3, 4 or 5—and if there was some hesitation about the matter he can be pretty certain it was 5. He sees the card drawn and can reckon within limits what the player's point now is. Suppose the banker's point is 4, and the punter draws a 9. The latter's point must now be either 9, 0, 1, 2, 3, or 4. It is obvious that the punter has only one chance of winning (i.e. if his point is 9). So the banker would "stand" with a considerable prospect of success.

If a player does not draw, and the banker's point is 4, he knows he is beaten unless he is fortunate enough to draw a five or under. The odds are against this (8 to 5), and he would not draw unless he was equally badly beaten by the other side of the table. For he has to apply his judgment separately to the two representative players: and where he is certainly beaten on one side, but stands a fair chance on the other, he would not draw. The bets on one side of the table would more or less pay those on the other.

There are no variations of the play at Baccarat, but rules as to auctioning the bank, and betting the full amount of the bank, vary at different resorts.

In some cases it is the rule that "banco" (the term for betting the limit) may only be called on the first deal. At others it may be called at any time, but only once during the run of any one bank. The players next the dealer have first option, and the others after them in their turns.

Generally, a bank finishes automatically when the cards

are exhausted, that is, when there are less than ten cards left unused.

If the banker retires through "breaking" or otherwise, any punter may *continue* his bank (i.e. he does not have fresh cards, but takes on those left of the original packs); but he must put up either (1) the amount originally put up by the banker if the latter retires "broken", or (2) the amount that the banker takes away; but this amount must equal or exceed the original bank.

At some resorts the bank may be bought for a fixed sum at certain specified times, and persons wishing to "purchase" put their names on a waiting list from which they are selected in order.

The points which an intending player needs to be quite certain about are as follows: —

He must not bet out of turn, and cannot bet more than the uncovered balance of the bank.

He must not look at his cards until the dealer has announced either a "natural" or that he "gives".

He must immediately declare a "natural" if he finds he has one.

He must *not* draw if his point is six or seven.

He *must* draw if his point is four or under.

He may use his own judgment when his point is five but the odds are against him.

He must not declare his point, after a draw, until the dealer has declared his.

CHEMIN DE FER

BACCARAT CHEMIN DE FER differs only slightly from Baccarat Banque, but it is rather more popular. The main differences are as under: —

The players are not divided into "sides" against the dealer. One hand only is dealt for the punters, and the player betting the largest amount holds it.

The "bank" passes to the next player in rotation every time the banker loses. A banker may, however, at any time withdraw his bank, and in such a case the players in their turns may claim it if willing to put up as much as is in the bank at the time; or, failing this, it is auctioned to the highest bidder. When his turn comes to take the bank, a player may refuse if he wishes, and he is under no obligation as to the amount he must put up if he takes it. He may risk as much or as little as he likes.

While holding the bank, the dealer must, as at Baccarat Banque, leave all his winnings in—unless the full amount is not covered by the total bets: in which case he may withdraw the balance.

The other rules are also as at Baccarat Banque; and as the holder of the cards is playing for all the money staked by the punters he is bound by the usual convention to draw when his point is under five and to stand when it is six or seven; and may exercise his option when it is five.

But as the dealer is not playing against two "sides" he is not allowed by convention to exercise his judgment as to drawing, and is bound to follow a certain recognised procedure, which is usually set out on a little card as under:—

If the banker's point is	And the punter	The banker must
0, 1, or 2 .	Draws any card, or stands	Draw.
3 or 4 . .	Draws 10, 9, or 8 .	Stand.
	Draws 7, 6, 5, 4, 3, 2, or 1; or stands . . .	Draw.
5 . . .	Draws 10, 9, 8, 2, or 1 .	Stand.
	Draws 7, 6, 5, 4, 3; or stands . . .	Draw.
6 . . .	Draws 6 or 5 . .	Draw.
	Draws 10, 9, 8, 7, 4, 3, 2, or 1; or stands . .	Stand.
7 . . .	Draws any card, or stands	Stand.
8 or 9 . .	——	Declare natural.

By reason of this convention, the odds are not nearly so much in the banker's favour as at banque.

The secret of the game's popularity lies probably in the fact that every player gets a turn as banker, and there is no need for him to risk any more than he can well afford. There is no doubt that it is more exciting to be banker than one of the punters, although it is not quite clear why. The turn comes round fairly quickly, and thus a player who loses his bank at the first deal is not discouraged.

It is sometimes agreed that a banker who has had three wins in succession may withdraw from the bank a half of his winnings (not half of the whole bank), and where this rule is observed it adds a certain zest.

Whilst waiting for his turn as banker, a player must of course bet—at least on every third deal. Any player who attempted to do the majority of his gambling as banker would be called on to "retire".

COON-CAN

THIS is an excellent game for any number of players up to six. It sometimes goes by the name of "Rummy", or "Rum". Two ordinary packs of fifty-two cards are used, plus one Joker, shuffled well together.

The players cut for deal, highest dealing: Aces count low in the cut and the Joker lowest. Ten cards are dealt one by one to each player, and when the deal is complete, a card is turned face upwards beside the remainder of the pack, which is laid face down in the centre of the table.

The object of each player is to get rid of all his cards by laying out on the table pair-royals or running flushes of three cards. (A pair-royal is three cards of the same rank, e.g. three sixes: a running-flush is three cards of the same suit in numerical order, e.g. four, five and six of Hearts).

The player on the dealer's left plays first. He picks up either the faced-up card, or the unexposed card from the top of the pack—whichever he pleases. Having done this, he may lay out any pair-royals or running flushes he now holds. If he cannot, or does not wish to do this, he must throw out one of his cards to replace the card he has drawn, placing it face upwards beside the pack.

The next player in the usual rotation now draws a card, and lays out or discards as the case may be; and so on for all the other players.

When once some cards have been laid out by a player, those that follow him may, between drawing and discarding, add any cards from their hands to the combinations on the table, no matter who laid them out.

Thus if there are three fours on the table, and you have a four, you may add it to those. Or if there is a sequence of, say, nine, ten, Jack, and you have seven and eight of the same suit, you may add both of them.

The Joker of course may be made to represent any card. If it is laid out at the end of a sequence (e.g. six, seven,

FIG. 21.—A "fixed" Joker at Coon-can

Joker, representing six, seven, and eight) a player wishing to add to that sequence may move it to the other end if it suits him. For instance, in the case mentioned, a player holding three and four (of same suit) would move the Joker, so that the new sequence would be three, four, Joker, six, seven. The Joker can only be moved once, however: and if it is originally placed in the middle of a sequence it cannot be moved at all. Once moved, it is usually placed, as in Fig. 21, to indicate that it is "fixed".

Aces may count high or low, i.e. in a running-flush of one-two-three or Queen-King-Ace. Note that King-one-two is not a "run".

As soon as a player gets rid of all his cards the hand is at an end. The others show the cards they still hold and pay him one stake for each "pip". The Joker counts fifteen, the Aces eleven, court cards all as ten, and other cards by face value.

If no player gets "out" before the pack is exhausted the drawing must then all be done from the top of the discard pile: and the players *must* discard a *different* card every time. (Previously they were at liberty to discard the same card.)

Certain simple principles should be borne in mind when playing. If you cannot secure cards to make the desired combinations, you can at least reduce the "count" of your hand by discarding your high cards. The Joker is to some extent a dangerous card to hold, since it counts fifteen against you, but it can generally be used pretty soon—so should be held for a while.

You may, by observing what your opponents draw, be able to "baulk" one or more of them. If you see a player joyously grabbing a King from the discard pile, and you have a King, then you may keep him "looking" for a while by not discarding it until absolutely necessary.

Similarly, you should watch all the discards: it is of no use holding on to two Kings if all the other Kings have been thrown away, and are, therefore, somewhere amongst the discards where you have practically no hope of ever reaching them.

But the chief opportunity for the display of skill is in choosing the moment at which to "lay out". It is obvious that the sooner you lay out the sooner you give your opponents the opportunity of "adding" to the cards put down. Hence it is wise to hold your complete combinations in your hand for a while; but not too long—or somebody may suddenly lay out his whole hand and call upon you for stakes according to the "count" of your cards.

COLONEL

Why it should be "Colonel" is not at all apparent. The game is an adaptation of Coon-can for two players only. In America it is known as "Single-pack Rummy".

One ordinary pack is used, and no Joker. The players cut for deal, the non-dealer playing first. He may pick up either the exposed card or the one on the top of the pack (see Coon-can) and discards one face upwards in its place.

He may "lay out" his running-flushes and pair-royals whenever he likes, between picking up and discarding. As at Coon-can it pays to delay "laying-out"—but not *too* long.

There is, however, a variation from Coon-can in that a player may at any time "challenge" his opponent, who may accept or refuse the challenge. If he accepts, the hands are immediately shown, and he who has the lowest "count" (Aces and court cards count ten, others by face value) is the winner and may receive either (1) a stake for each point of difference between the hands, or (2) a stake for *every* point of the loser's hand (e.g. if loser's hand "counts" sixty-five and winner's forty-five, the latter would receive either twenty or sixty-five stakes). This matter should be agreed upon beforehand.

As soon as one of the players has laid out all his ten cards the game is of course at an end, and he receives stakes according to the "count" of the other player's cards.

The general principles of winning play are:—

A pair-royal or running-flush of "ten" point cards should be laid out as soon as possible, to avoid being "caught" with them still in hand. Also, running-flushes, open only at one end, may be laid out early, as only one card can be "added" (e.g. one-two-three or Queen-King-Ace). King, Ace, two does not *run*, by the way.

Low pair-royals and sequences should be held for some time.

If you cannot get sequences or pair-royals, secure low cards by the exchange and "challenge".

OLD MAID

THIS is a favourite game for the family circle and is much enjoyed by youngsters. A Queen is abstracted from an ordinary pack, which is then dealt round (one card at a time) to the players. Up to eight or nine can play.

Each player inspects his hand and discards any "pairs" (e.g. two fours) to the centre of the table, without exposing them. This done, the player on the dealer's left offers his hand, spread fan-wise, backs uppermost, to his left-hand neighbour, who must take one card. If this pairs with one he holds, he throws out the pair. If not, he adds the card to his hand; and offers it in the same manner to the next player, who does as already described. This goes on until gradually one by one all the players manage to pair and throw away their cards—excepting one, who will be found holding the odd Queen. He or she, it is said, will be the "bachelor", or "old maid".

HEARTS

HEARTS is rather an ingenious game which may not in-accurately be described as "Whist upside-down". The play resembles Whist except for two important details, viz.: —

(1) There are no trumps; but hearts are the opposite thing to trumps, being the cards you hate to get and which you discard at every opportunity.

(2) In play, you aim to avoid taking any trick which contains a Heart.

Players must follow suit; and the penalty for a revoke, if revoker loses, is that he must pay up for the other losers: and if he wins, he must put his winnings into the pool.

There are usually no partners, play being each against the rest.

At the end of each hand, the players show the Hearts which are in the tricks they have taken. He with none, or the lowest number, receives from each of the others one stake for every Heart card that he (the loser) holds, to-gether with the pool, if any.

Another method of staking is for each player to put one stake into the pool every time he takes a Heart.

If two or more players hold an equal number of Hearts at the end of the hand, they divide the winnings received from players with a higher number. Any odd stake is left in the pool for the next hand.

The game is sometimes played by partners, and in this variation there is considerable scope for good play. Whist principles, *inverted*, crop up in many ways. For instance, instead of leading a suit for your partner to trump you lead it for him to discard his Hearts upon. Again, the

E

stronger you and your partner are in Hearts the greater is the necessity to avoid a lead of Hearts.

"Hearts" well repays a little practice and study, and is by no means a child's game.

PELMANISM

PELMANISM is named after the inimitable "Pelman Institute", and, as may be guessed, is a "memory" game.

An ordinary full pack is spread out by single cards, backs uppermost, on the table—not too regularly arranged.

The players, of whom there may be any reasonable number, take it in turn to lift any two of the cards, show them, and replace them in the same positions. If, however, the cards are a pair, the player removes them to a heap in front of him, and they count as a trick to him.

The essence of the game lies in remembering where particular cards are, so that when you raise your first card you may know where to go for its fellow and thus secure a trick.

At the beginning it is fairly easy to remember where three or four cards are, but as the game proceeds one is apt to get a little "mixed".

The player securing most pairs (or "tricks") wins.

It is a good game for children, who can generally beat their elders at it.

SPECULATION

SPECULATION is another good family game, and is played as follows: —

Three cards are dealt from a full ordinary pack to each player. Any reasonable number may play. Before dealing the dealer puts a stake into the pool, and all other players must put half the amount of such stake (e.g. he puts two counters, the others one each). When the deal is complete the next card is turned up as trumps. The object of each player is to secure the highest trump. If the turn-up is an

Ace, it belongs to the dealer, and he wins the pool, the hand being at an end.

If the turn-up is not an Ace, but is fairly high, the dealer will offer it for sale, and anyone who desires to "speculate" may do so, the highest bidder securing the card. He places it face upwards on top of his hand.

No player is allowed to look at his cards until his turn comes, and then he may only see one. After the turn-up has been dealt with, the eldest hand turns up his first card. If it is not a higher trump than the turn-up, the next player turns up a card: and so on until a trump which beats the turn-up appears. The player who for the time being has the highest trump in front of him does not turn up his cards. A higher trump having appeared (the appearance of the Ace of trumps of course ends the hand), it is at once auctioned, the successful bidder paying his "price" into the pool, or to the player from whose hand it comes, whichever method is agreed upon.

A player may at any time offer a price for any card exposed or unexposed, or he may buy two cards, or a whole hand.

It is imperative if counters are used to give them a small money value—at so much the dozen. "Speculation" is rife, and bidding runs high towards the end of a hand, and unless there is some financial check on the players the "prices" may become rather absurd.

NEWMARKET

THIS is a remarkably simple game, yet it is full of exciting possibilities. Any number of players may take part; but we think that three to five is the most suitable number.

Before play commences, each participant is given an equal number of counters or, if playing for money, the stakes are agreed upon. Then, from a spare pack, the Ace of Spades, the King of Hearts, the Queen of Clubs and the Knave of Diamonds are taken and placed in square formation in the middle of the table.

Next, a dealer is agreed upon for the first round and subsequent rounds are dealt by the player seated to the left of the previous dealer.

Before the cards have been shuffled and dealt, each player lays his stakes. For this an ordinary player uses four, eight or twelve counters; but the dealer lays twice as many as anybody else. The counters are placed on any of the four cards mentioned above. An equal share may be put on each of the cards, several on some and few on others, or all on one, just as fancy dictates. In making the stakes, no skill is involved and this part of the game is purely a matter of whim.

The stakes being laid, the full pack of cards is dealt out, the first card going to the person on the left of the dealer, while a dummy hand is dealt to the centre of the table. Sometimes, the cards of this hand are placed face upwards; but it adds to the skill if they are not seen.

Having arranged all the preliminaries, the player on the left of the dealer lays the lowest card he has of any suit he chooses. The player to his left is then given the opportunity of following with the next higher card of the same suit, and so the game continues until somebody cannot go because the card necessary to follow on is in the dummy hand. This condition is called a "stop".

When a "stop" occurs, the person who played the "stop" leads afresh from any suit he chooses and play is resumed until, at last, somebody has no more cards. Such person is the winner of the game, and the other players must pay him one counter for every card they still hold.

As every card is laid, it must be audibly named; and note that the Ace is the lowest card.

Perhaps it may be thought that Newmarket is a game fit only for small children; but there is a great deal in playing it well. The first essential is to remember what is played and, unless this can be done, a success will never be made. To illustrate this point, let us suppose that someone commences with a five of Diamonds and the run continues with a six, seven, eight, nine and then a "stop" comes. Also, let us suppose that the four of Diamonds is in your hand. See how important it is to remember that your four is a "stop" card. At any time, when you happen to have the lead, the four may be played alone and you can lead again.

Naturally, the "stops" increase in number as the game proceeds and more and more concentration is needed to remember them all.

The best cards to hold are sequences of runs, especially those terminating with a King, since this is the highest card of a suit and must, necessarily, be a "stop". The value of a sequence lies in the fact that it enables a player to get rid of several cards at a time. Next to a sequence, it is best to hold cards that run alternately, because, here again, there is a chance of parting with them rapidly.

So far, we have not explained the reason for the four "lay-out" cards and the stakes put to them. They are used in this way: As soon as a player lays one of these cards from his hand, he is entitled to all the stakes put to it. It should be, perhaps, recalled that the "lay-out" cards are not taken from the playing pack, but are "spares" from another.

One thing remains. Suppose that the dummy hand contains one or more of the four "lay-out" cards. When this occurs, nobody can claim the stakes put to these particular cards. How to dispose of the stakes, then? The usual plan is to shuffle the full pack and for the last dealer to deal out the cards again, face upwards, omitting the dummy hand. Whoever happens to have a card, on which there is unclaimed stake-money, takes it.

PART II

PATIENCE GAMES

INTRODUCTION

PATIENCE is so deservedly popular as to warrant its inclusion in any book of card games. As its American name, "Solitaire", indicates, it is primarily designed for one player: and in this form it is a welcome pastime to all those who are compelled to spend long periods alone. There are, however, many games which may be played by two or more players in competition.

In all descriptions of Patience games there are certain terms in constant use with which a learner must be acquainted. Those most frequently used are: —

Base-card, or Foundation. The card which forms the foundation of a packet; generally, but not invariably, an Ace.

Building up. Placing cards on the base-packets.

Column. Cards disposed perpendicularly. In close column they overlap one another, in open column they are slightly apart.

Chockered or Blocked. The cards being so blocked, or "sealed", that they cannot be used.

Exposed Cards. Cards at the bottom of the columns; those which have none below them, or cards at the end of a row.

Family. All the cards of the same suit.

Fan. The cards disposed in open formation resembling a fan; the upper card is the exposed one.

Grace. The privilege of one illegal move when a game is blocked.

High Cards. From eight to the King.

Index Row. A row which is not to be packed on.

Lay-out. The first disposition of a game.

Marriage. Two cards of consecutive value placed together.

Packing. Placing cards on the exposed ones in the lay-out.

Row. Cards disposed horizontally.

Rubbish, or Waste-heap. A packet composed of those cards which cannot be placed either on the base-packets or on the exposed ones in the lay-out.

Sealed. Cards or packets which are placed face down: or which are covered by other cards.

Sequence. Cards following one another in numerical order, but not necessarily in suit.

Ascending Sequence. A sequence progressing from low to high (e.g. Ace to King).

Descending Sequence. One progressing from high to low (e.g. King to Ace).

Main Sequence. The final arrangement to be secured by "building".

Auxiliary Sequence. Temporary sequences made in course of play, by "packing".

Stock. A number of cards counted out to begin with, and placed in a packet by themselves to be used as directed; or, the cards that are left "in hand" after the "lay-out" has been made.

Talon. Another name for stock.

Vacancy. An empty space made in the lay-out.

Waiving. Lifting a card, and using the one beneath it.

Worrying back. Returning the cards from the base-packets to the lay-out.

The ultimate aim of practically all Patience games is to arrange the cards in a certain definite order, usually complete sequences of suits.

In some games single packs of fifty-two cards are used, in others two or more packs are required. The two-pack games are generally the more intricate, but many of them have the disadvantage of requiring a fairly large space for the "lay-out".

Small "Patience packs" can be bought, and are much preferable in a case where Patience is regularly played.

The "Chastleton" board is useful for invalid Patience players who cannot sit up to a table. These boards are quite cheap and simple: the "lay-out" cards are kept in position by elastic bands, and there are suitable recesses for "stock" and other packets.

It is only possible to include in this book a small number of the very many Patience games now played, but an effort has been made to make the selection as representative as possible of the various types.

Those who wish to explore further should obtain one of the many books devoted solely to Patience.

"ROLL-CALL" PATIENCE (one pack)

THIS is a most simple game; it is an excellent way of teaching children the names of the cards and of keeping them occupied for a while.

An ordinary pack is dealt one at a time face upwards on to the waste-heap, the player meanwhile calling the names of the cards in rotation, thus "Ace, two, three, four, five," and so on, up to King and on to "Ace, two, three," etc., again. When a card "answers its name" (i.e. comes at the same time) it is thrown out. The game continues until all are thrown out, or until they "won't answer". It is purely chance which decides.

"THE TRAVELLERS" PATIENCE (one pack)

DEAL the cards, face down, into three rows of four, until there are only four cards left. These are placed by themselves, also face down, a little to the left of the bottom row, and are called "the travellers".

In play you have to imagine that the twelve packets of four are numbered one to twelve, as in Fig. 22.

First turn up the top card of "the travellers" and place it face up, underneath its proper packet (i.e. a two under No. 2, a nine under No. 9, a Jack or Queen under No. 11 or No. 12). There is no packet for Kings, and these are placed by themselves a little to the right of the bottom row. Suppose a four is first turned up: you place it under No. 4, and then turn up the top card of that packet, and place it where it belongs, turning up the top card of *that* packet, and so on. Whenever a King appears you have to turn up another "traveller".

If all four travellers are turned up before every card is in its proper place the game is blocked.

Fig. 22 shows a game in progress.

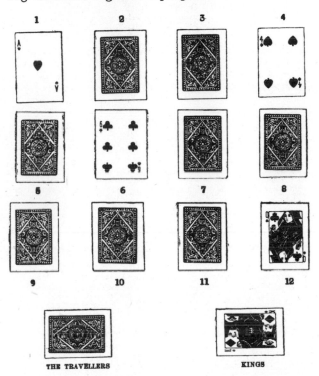

Fig. 22.—"The Travellers" Patience in progress

"TOWER OF HANOY" PATIENCE (one pack)

This, by way of a change, is a game of pure skill, and is more in the nature of a mathematical puzzle than real Patience. It is, in fact, an adaptation of an old puzzle.

Only nine cards are used; they should be of one suit, from the two to the ten inclusive. They are laid out in three rows of three, as shown in Fig. 23.

The object is to get them into a single column in descending sequence by moving according to the following rules:—

One card only may be moved at a time.

It must be a card from the foot of a column.

It can only be placed at the foot of another column and *below a higher card*.

When a "vacancy" occurs (i.e. when all in one column have been moved) the bottom card of either of the remaining columns may be used to fill the vacancy.

FIG. 23.—"Tower of Hanoy" Patience

In the example shown in Fig. 23 it will be seen that the ten cannot be moved at all, at first. It must be got into the top row as soon as possible. Here are the moves:—

4 under 10, 7 under 9, 5 under 7, 4 under 5; then 10 into vacancy.

The next process is to get the nine under the ten, which is not so easy.

The game is an excellent pastime, and generally a little more thought will solve the most hopeless looking "block".

"SIR TOMMY" PATIENCE (one pack)

THIS is a very old Patience, which looks simple but can be very obstinate at times.

The object is to build up ascending sequences (Ace up to King) irrespective of suit. The cards are dealt face upwards into four heaps, and you may place each card as it is dealt on *any* of the heaps. As the Aces appear they are

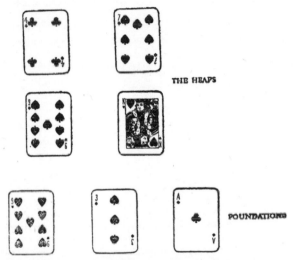

THE HEAPS

FOUNDATIONS

FIG. 24.—"Sir Tommy" Patience in progress

placed in a row below the heaps, and whenever a card appears which will build on to them in sequence it is of course so built, and not put on to a heap, unless there is some advantage in doing so.

The difficulty lies in deciding where to put the cards which will not go on to the base packets (foundations), for the exposed card of each heap is always available for building on the main sequences, and if you put a high card on a low one you risk "blocking" it.

Try, as far as possible, to keep the heaps for cards of approximately the same value, i.e. one for high, one for "not so high", one for medium, one for low.

It is not permissible to move cards from one heap to another.

The game is lost if the sequences are not complete before the cards of the stock are all dealt on to the heaps. Fig. 24 shows a game in progress.

"DEMON" PATIENCE (one pack)

THIS is a very popular but rather difficult game to conclude successfully.

A packet of thirteen cards is first dealt and placed face upwards (the top card only showing) on the table. The

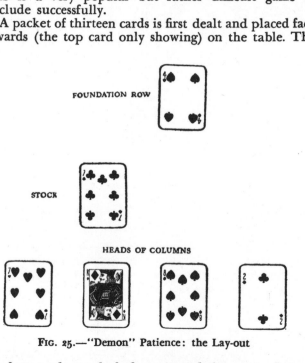

FIG. 25.—"Demon" Patience: the Lay-out

next four cards are dealt face upwards in a row clear of this packet (which is called the "stock" or "talon"). A further card is dealt and forms the first of a row of "foundations" above these rows. Other cards of the same value are placed beside it when they appear.

The remainder of the pack is kept in hand, and cards are turned up from it *in threes* on to a waste-heap.

The object is to build on the foundations in ascending sequence of suit. In the play the first four single cards laid out form the heads of columns to be "packed" upon in *descending* sequence in *alternate colours*. The top card of the stock and of the waste-heap is always available for building, and any sequence or bottom part of a sequence may be moved from one column to another. The exposed

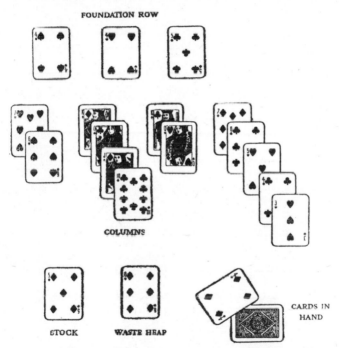

FIG. 26.—"Demon" Patience in progress

(bottom) cards of columns are of course available for building the main sequences.

Fig. 25 shows the lay-out: Fig 26 shows the game in progress wherein the four of Diamonds may be moved to the foundation row. On this the top card of stock can be placed, followed by top card of Waste-heap. Part of the auxiliary sequence in the right-hand column can be moved to the left-hand column, thus releasing six of Clubs for the main sequence.

When no exposed card or auxiliary sequence can be moved with advantage three more cards are turned up on to the waste-heap from the cards in hand. When all these have been so turned up, the waste-heap is turned over (*once* only) and dealt in threes as before. If the game is blocked you are allowed one "grace", viz. to move *one* card from a foundation packet (main sequence) to the head or foot of a column, if it will fit. If this does not get you "out" the game is lost.

"TRIANGLE" PATIENCE (two packs)

THE two packs are shuffled well together. Deal out a row of ten cards, nine face down and the tenth face up: then a row of nine, eight face down and the ninth face up: and continue so dealing, one card less per row each time until one card face up forms the bottom of the triangle.

The cards may overlap the cards above them.

The *"packing"* is done in *descending* sequence of *alternate colours*. When an exposed card is moved, the sealed card above it may be turned up. When a vacancy is made in the top row, the exposed card or sequence from the column adjoining the vacancy, on the left, is moved up into it. Aces as they appear are placed apart as foundations, and *built on* in *ascending* sequence of *suit*. A sequence, or bottom part of one, may be moved on to a card which it fits.

When no more "packing" or "building" from the lay-out can be done, the stock (cards in hand) is dealt to a waste-heap one by one. The top card of the waste-heap is always available for packing. The waste-heap cannot be turned and dealt again. If the game is blocked one "grace" is allowed, viz. a card may be moved from a "base-packet" (main sequence) on to an auxiliary sequence, if this is of any use.

Fig. 27 shows the lay-out, with one foundation laid: it will be seen that several cards can be "packed", viz. Clubs ten on to Hearts Jack, then Diamonds nine, and then stop: Clubs five on to Diamonds six, followed by Hearts four. This makes a vacancy to be filled by Diamonds Queen. This leaves five cards to be turned up, as the Ace of Spades was moved from the bottom of the triangle to form the first foundation.

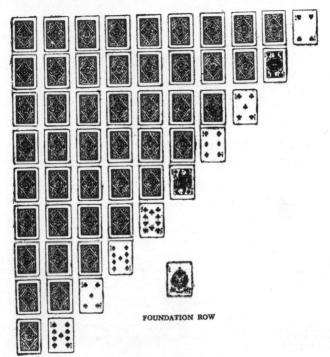

FOUNDATION ROW

FIG. 27.—"Triangle" Patience: the Lay-out

"MISS MILLIGAN" PATIENCE (two packs)

THIS is a very old favourite, and is practically the same as "Triangle". The two packs being shuffled, eight cards are dealt out in a row face upwards. Any Aces that appear are placed as foundations above the row, and built on in ascending sequence of suits. Packing on the first cards dealt is done in descending sequence and alternate colours. When all packing and building possible has been done with the first row another row of eight is dealt across, which "seals" or closes the cards above it: only the *bottom* cards of columns are "exposed cards".

When a vacancy is made in a row only a King, or sequence headed by a King, may be moved into it—and

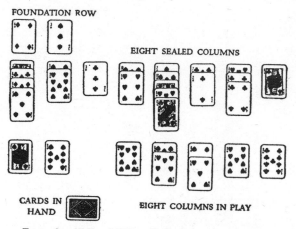

FOUNDATION ROW

EIGHT SEALED COLUMNS

CARDS IN HAND

EIGHT COLUMNS IN PLAY

FIG. 28.—"Miss Milligan" Patience in progress

this is what makes the game difficult (in "Triangle" you may move *any* card to a vacancy).

There is no waste-heap, all the cards in hand being dealt in rows of eight. If the game is blocked there is one privilege—you may "waive" *one* card from the foot of a column; i.e. hold it suspended while you move cards underneath it, until you find a suitable place for it. If this fails, the game is lost.

Fig. 28 shows a game in progress, in which several movements can be made.

"SULTAN" PATIENCE (two packs)

THE final arrangement of this represents the King of Hearts surrounded by his harem of eight Queens. For the lay-out first place the Ace of Hearts and the eight Kings

Then deal on each side of this group four cards as shown: these are called the "Divan".

The central King of Hearts is not built upon. The Ace of Hearts and the other Kings are built on in ascending

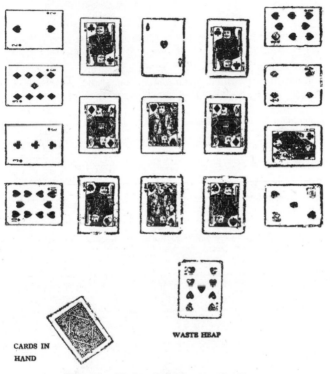

CARDS IN
HAND

WASTE HEAP

FIG. 29.—"Sultan" Patience: the Lay-out

sequence of suit—on Kings beginning with the Ace, and on the Ace of Hearts with the two.

The cards in hand are dealt singly to a waste-heap, the top card of which is always available for building. Cards of the "Divan" are also always available, and where one is used a new one is immediately dealt in its place or taken from the waste-heap. There is no "packing" or "auxiliary sequences".

There are no privileges or "graces", but the waste-heap may be turned *twice*.

"STAR" PATIENCE (two packs)

FOR the "lay-out" place the King of Hearts in the centre (the other seven Kings are not used at all) and arrange the eight Aces round it, as shown in Fig. 30. Then deal a card outside each of the Aces. If any twos appear place

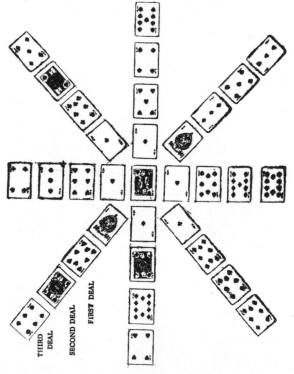

FIG. 30.—"Star" Patience in progress

them on their proper Aces and deal another card to fill the vacancy. All possible building in ascending suit sequence on the Aces having been done, deal cards round the points of the star as shown in the illustration. More building can probably be done, and vacancies should be filled from the pack. Then a final deal of cards is made to form the outer points of the star. From these, further building can be done, and in addition "marriages" may be made of these outer cards (in descending suit sequence).

The cards in hand are then dealt on to the waste-heap, top card of which is always available for marriage or building. If you can open one of the rays as far as the Ace, you may fill up with exposed (outermost) cards from other rays.

The final arrangement is the King of Hearts, surrounded by eight Queens; but this is a difficult Patience, and does not often "come out".

Fig. 31 shows a completed game.

FIG. 31.—"Star" Patience completed

"BIG WHEEL" PATIENCE (two packs)

LAY out the eight Kings in a circle as shown in Fig. 32. Then, outside each King, as shown, place a packet of four cards face upwards.

If the top card of any of these packets is Ace, two, or three, it should be placed in its proper position (inside King of same suit), as indicated in Fig. 33.

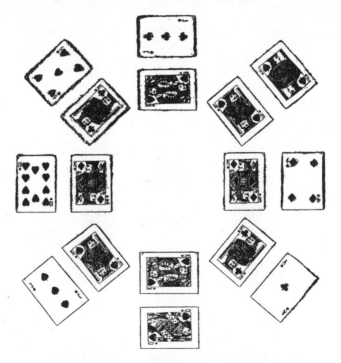

FIG. 32.—"Big Wheel" Patience: the Lay-out

The twos and threes are the "base cards", and on them you build *in suit* by *alternate numbers*: i.e. on a two you place four, six, eight, ten, Queen, and on a three you place five, seven, nine, Jack.

Before dealing from cards in hand, do any building possible; if and when one of the outside packets of four is exhausted, a new packet of four is dealt in its place.

Deal one by one to a waste-heap, building on founda-

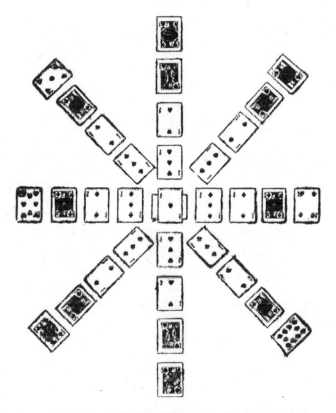

FIG. 33.—"Big Wheel" Patience in progress

tions where possible, and renewing outside packets where necessary. If the top card of a packet is same as the top card of waste-heap, and there is a place for one of them, the card from the packet *must* be used.

When all cards are dealt, "packing" in ascending *or* descending sequence of *suit* on the outside packets may be done, to relieve cards "sealed" in the packets. The waste-heap cannot be turned.

The successful conclusion is shown in Fig. 34.

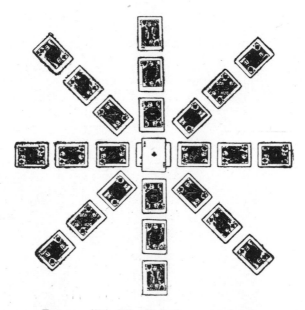

FIG. 34.—"Big Wheel" Patience completed.

"EMPEROR" PATIENCE (two packs)

THIS is rather more intricate than the preceding games, and is considered by many to be one of the best games of Patience yet invented.

First lay out a row of ten packets of three cards face downwards. Next, underneath them, lay a row of single cards face upwards. As Aces appear, at any time during the game, they are placed by themselves below or to one side to form base cards, and are built upon in ascending

sequence of suit. "Packing" is done on the exposed cards
of the second row, columns being formed in descending
sequence and alternate colours. Fig. 35 shows a game in
progress.

The sealed packets of the top row cannot be touched
until there is a vacancy in the row immediately beneath
(i.e. when a column has disappeared). When this occurs,
however, the top card of the sealed packet may be turned
up and considered as filling the vacancy. The cards in
hand are dealt to the waste-heap one by one. The top card

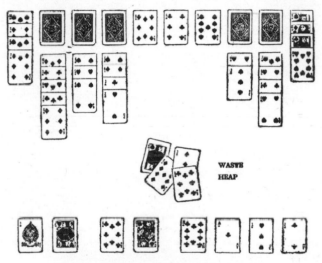

FIG. 35.—"Emperor" Patience in progress

of the waste-heap is always available for packing or building. Exposed cards, or sequences, or bottom parts of
sequences may be moved from one column to another, if
they will fit. Further, cards which have been built on to
the main sequences (base cards), may be taken off again
and "packed" on columns to relieve a block. This is an
unusual privilege and is called "worrying back". It is
frequently necessary to do it more than once, before the
player, supposing he is fortunate, succeeds in concluding
with eight complete suits headed by a King.

"ST. HELENA" PATIENCE (two packs)

THIS game is said to have been invented, or at any rate played, by Napoleon to relieve the monotony of his confinement at St. Helena.

The two packs are not shuffled together, but used separately. First lay out four Kings and four Aces, as

FIG. 36.—"St. Helena" Patience: the Lay-out

shown in Fig. 36: then deal twelve cards round the outside of the Kings and Aces, as illustrated.

The Aces are to be built upon *upwards* and the Kings *downwards*, in suit. The four cards on the right and left of the lay-out may be used to build on any Ace or King; but the eight cards in the top and bottom rows may only be used to build upon the Ace or King they happen to adjoin. Into any vacancy made (by building) in the outside cards a new card is at once dealt. When no more building can be done, eight more cards are dealt round outside on top of the first eight; and all possible building is done from these—always observing the rule which limits building from the top and bottom rows to the adjacent King or Ace.

The second pack is dealt through similarly to the first, but in this of course Kings and Aces will appear: they are not laid out specially as are those of the first pack.

When both packs have been dealt out the restrictions are temporarily removed and a card from *any* outside packet may be built on *any* foundation.

Also, cards may be moved from one outside packet to another to form "marriages" in either upward or down-

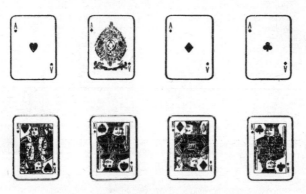

FIG. 37.—"St. Helena" Patience completed

ward sequences (i.e. a seven of Hearts may be placed on six of Hearts, or on eight of Hearts, whichever is most advantageous).

Having done the best you can by marrying, if the main sequences are not completed, as shown in Fig. 37, you may pick up the outside packets *in the reverse order to that in which they were dealt round*, and after placing them one on top of the other, face upwards, go through the whole dealing process again (subject to the same limitations). At the end of this deal restrictions are again relaxed and marriages may be made.

A third deal may be made if necessary (it generally is), and restrictions relaxed and marriages made again at the end: but if this fails, the game is lost.

"DOMINO" PATIENCE
(for three or more players)

THIS game is sometimes known by the simple name of "Sevens".

An ordinary pack is dealt round in the ordinary way to the players. The eldest hand must play a seven or pass; if he passes, the next player must play a seven or pass; and so on. When a seven is played, the next player may place beside it a card in ascending or descending sequence of suit (i.e. a six or eight). Other players may continue the sequences, pass, or play another seven.

Thus the game goes on until one player has got rid of

FIG. 38.—"Domino" Patience in progress

all his cards. He is the winner, and usually receives a stake for each card still held by each of the other players.

Three or four players make the best game: and after a few games it will become apparent that the most skilful player always wins.

The art lies in "holding up" your opponents. It should be said that if you hold a card in sequence, or a seven, you *must* play it: but you frequently have a choice—and an unwise choice is easy to make.

"Middle" cards in sequence are the best to hold: thus if you hold six, seven, eight, and nine of a suit you can have two "free goes" as they are called, viz. the seven and eight.

The playing of these does not "let out" any other cards, and if you can manage to play others and hold on to the six and nine till towards the end of the game you will probably win.

The other players who hold the cards of the same suit above nine and below six can do nothing but pass in that suit until you lay one of them. Fig. 38 shows a game in progress.

"HOLIDAY" PATIENCE
(for three or more players)

AN ordinary pack is dealt round face down in front of the players. They do not inspect their hands. The last card is turned up and placed in the centre of the table to form the beginning of a row: let us suppose it is an eight.

The first player turns up his top card. If it will "build" in upward sequence (e.g. a nine) he places it *beside* the

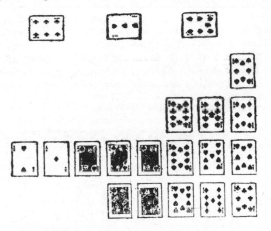

FIG. 39.—"Holiday" Patience in progress

eight irrespective of suit. If it happens to be another eight he places it below the first. Otherwise the turn passes on.

Each turns up all his cards one by one, building where he can, and putting others on to a waste-heap, face upwards.

All players have the added advantage of being able to "pack", in upward or downward sequence, on any other player's waste-heap. Each must, however, play to the lay-out if he can: and if he plays on to an opponent's waste-heap when there is an opportunity to "build", he must stop and wait until his next turn.

Thus play goes on, waste-heaps being turned over and played through again when necessary, until one player wins by getting rid of all his cards.

Fig. 39 shows a game in progress.

"BATTLE" PATIENCE (for two players)

EACH player has a full pack. Taking turns, they deal the cards into thirteen packets of four each, i.e. as though dealing to thirteen players, but face upwards. Whenever a card falls in its "right" place—that is to say when a seven falls on the seventh packet, or a King on the thirteenth—it is set aside.

After the first deal the packets are gathered up, well shuffled and dealt again in the same way, more cards, if the player is lucky, being set aside.

At the end of four deals, each player shows the cards which have fallen in their right places, and scores points for them according to their "numbers", viz. from Aces, one, to King, thirteen.

Fig. 40 shows a game in progress.

FIRST PLAYER'S
SCORING CARDS

SECOND PLAYER'S
SCORING CARDS

FIG. 40.—"Battle" Patience in progress

"CRIBBAGE" PATIENCE
(for two or more players)

THIS is an excellent game, and may also be played by the solitary player.

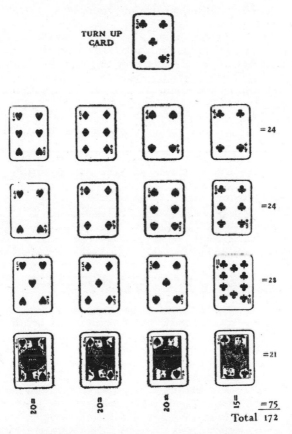

FIG. 41.—"Cribbage" Patience: a hand which scores 172

Each player has his own pack. He deals sixteen cards (the pack being held back uppermost) and looks at each card as it is dealt. He has to place them in four rows of four cards, and must observe the following rules. The first card having been laid down face upwards, the next card must be placed adjacent to it—either above, below, on either side, or corner to corner. The next card is placed adjacent to the first two in the same way; but it must be remembered that the final lay-out must be a square (four cards each way).

When all sixteen have been placed another card is placed by the side as the "turn-up"; and then the cards are reckoned according to six-card cribbage rules. (Cribbage players will have no difficulty in understanding this; those who do not should refer to the section on Cribbage, page 75.)

The lay-out comprises eight hands—four across and four vertically—with each of which the turn-up is of course counted.

The art of the game is in deciding how to place the cards as they are dealt out—and there is opportunity for considerable skill in this.

The maximum score is 172, as shown in Fig. 42.

If the turn-up is a Jack it is not usual to score "two for his heels", but a Jack in the lay-out, of the same suit as the turn-up, of course scores "one for his nob".

"BUBBLY" PATIENCE

This is a very jolly game for any number of players, but especially for six to ten. Each player is given a full pack of fifty-two cards, which should preferably have very different backs, so that sorting may be facilitated.

The game begins by the players putting down four cards each. These should be taken from the top of the shuffled pack and arranged in a horizontal line on the table. The cards are face-up and conveniently near to the owners. A little to the right of the line, thirteen further cards are placed, all face-up, and taken from the pack in order. These cards are called the stock.

When each player has arranged his own lay-out, the word "Go" is called, and then the game is to race through the various operations as rapidly as possible, since every second counts.

These are the steps that have to be performed:

(a) Any face-up Ace has to be placed in the centre of the table and there is no need to keep one player's Ace separate from those of other players.

(b) Upon the Aces, the cards have to be built upwards to the Kings, in consecutive order and of the same suit. Anybody can play on any of these cards in the centre of the table.

(c) On the four cards forming the initial horizontal row, the owner builds downwards in consecutive order and alternate colours. The cards for this are taken (i) from the initial four, (ii) from the top of the stock, or (iii) from the remainder of the pack. The latter is turned over three cards at a time and any face card may be used. The pack, it should be explained, may be run through any number of times while play continues in progress. Note that the row of four cards may be built on by the owner only.

As soon as a player has replaced all his cards in the centre, he calls "Out!" and the first to make this call is the winner.

Some people count the number of wins gained by each player, and others go by points. In the latter case, the first to call "Out" takes ten points for winning, plus two points for every card he has built up on the Aces. The other players take two points for each card so placed.

From this description, it will be seen that the quick player has an enormous advantage. Should two people wish to build up the same card on the Ace packs, it is the first to lay his card that places it: the other must wait for a subsequent opportunity.

"IDIOT'S DELIGHT"

THIS is one of the most fascinating games of Patience. It is played with one pack.

First, put out nine cards, face upwards, in a horizontal line: then, below, put out eight, so that the ninth space is empty. Follow by putting out seven, six, five . .

down to one card. In the last row, there will be one card and eight empty spaces. This accounts for forty-five cards and there will be seven left over. Spread these out, face upwards, on the right of the triangle.

Now, you are allowed to manœuvre with the bottom card of any vertical row and with the seven spares: but no others.

Your aim is to work the cards about so that you can reach the Aces and abstract them from the lay-out, building up on them in ascending order of the same suits.

The moves, however, must be made according to rule. The bottom card of one file can be placed on the bottom card of any other file as long as it is of a value of one less and of the opposite colour; and, of course, the bottom card can be taken from the lay-out to build up on the four Aces, if a card already on the building stocks is one less in value and of the same suit.

It must be noted that only one card may be moved at a time, except when a complete vertical file is empty. Then, the bottom pile of cards of any other vertical row may be put there.

The seven spares are used for building up on the Aces, when the occasion permits; but their greatest use is in helping to build on the bottom cards of the vertical files. For instance, suppose there is a black four and a black six among these bottom cards and a red five happens to be one of the spares. The five can go on the six and, then, the four may be moved and, in moving it, perhaps you are bringing into play some other card that is very helpful.